ONE HUNDRED YEARS OF
MEDICAL MURDER

One Hundred Years of
Medical Murder

JOHN CAMP

THE BODLEY HEAD
LONDON SYDNEY
TORONTO

ACKNOWLEDGEMENTS

Thanks are due to the following for permission to reproduce photographs: the Mary Evans Picture Library (no. 1); the Mansell Collection (no. 2); the Royal College of Physicians (no. 3); Syndication International (no. 4); Agence Roger-Viollet, Paris (nos. 10-13, 15); B.B.C. Hulton Picture Library (no. 14); Flicks Photograph Library (nos 17 and 18). Nos 5-9 and no. 16 are from the author's collection

British Library Cataloguing
in Publication Data
Camp, John
One Hundred Years of Medical Murder
1. Murder   2. Physicians
I. Title
364. 1'523 HV 6513
ISBN 0-370-30354-7

© John Camp 1982
Printed in Great Britain for
The Bodley Head Ltd
9 Bow Street, London, WC2E 7AL
by Redwood Burn Ltd
Trowbridge, Wiltshire
Set in Garamond
First Published 1982

CONTENTS

1

William Palmer

(1824-1856)

There was a time when the phrase 'criminal classes' was frequently heard in any discussion of social problems. It conjured up a vision of a degenerate section of the community, poor, dirty, and ill-housed, even with a cast of countenance popularly supposed to be indicative of criminal tendencies. Today we hear the expression far less, for experience has shown that there is no such thing as 'a criminal class' and that felons and wrong-doers come from every section of the community. Indeed, the history of major crime, and of murder in particular, indicates that it is frequently the more affluent who resort to ingenious methods of ridding themselves of unwanted friends or relatives.

Three of the most successful multiple murderers in history were not only medical practitioners, but also wealthy ones. In France during the Second World War, Dr Marcel Petiot, already a substantial property-owner, was convicted of organizing a bogus 'escape route' for rich Jews, killing them and retaining their money and possessions. In late Victorian London Dr Neill Cream murdered a number of prostitutes, apparently with no motive other than the simple enjoyment of killing. He, too, was a well-educated man with plenty of money, proud of his expertise and glorying in the fact that he could remain one jump ahead of the police despite the clues he gave them. In the early years of Queen Victoria's reign there was the extraordinary case of Dr William Palmer, of Rugeley, near Stafford. Initially possessed of a considerable fortune, Palmer squandered his money on gambling and resorted to murder in an attempt to pay off his racing debts and avoid the scandal of a trial for fraud and forgery.

All these men were of high intelligence, they came from backgrounds where poverty was unknown, and yet each ended his life on the gallows, convicted of the most cold-blooded murders. Under these circumstances, what can be defined as 'the criminal classes'?

A study of William Palmer's immediate forbears may be revealing. A criminal streak had been present in his family for several generations. His maternal grandfather's fortune had been gained by consistently defrauding a wealthy widow over many years and finally jilting her. Palmer's mother, the issue of this liaison, had married the owner of a flourishing sawmill whose income had been greatly augmented by the theft of timber from the nearby estate of the Marquess of Anglesey. This had been achieved largely through the connivance of the estate bailiff, who later became one of Mrs Palmer's many lovers. In fact, her promiscuity became so well-known in Rugeley that there was some doubt about the exact paternity of her seven children, two girls and five boys.

Not all the children inherited these criminal tendencies. True, one of her daughters grew up to become a 'fallen woman' but managed to fall on her feet in the process, eventually marrying a wealthy widower, and Walter, the eldest son, would almost certainly have drunk himself to death had he not been speeded on his way by his brother William. But the rest of the family, once they had moved away from Rugeley, lived respectable lives, and as a result were never heard of again. It was William, the second son, who was to bring notoriety to the family name.

William Palmer was born in 1824. He was a bright child, and enjoyed school though his reports constantly referred to his laziness. Like many clever children he found he could do the work without too much mental effort and devoted the remainder of his energies to the avoidance of any extra duties.

At the age of sixteen he was apprenticed to the famous Liverpool firm of manufacturing chemists, Evans & Co. Ltd. Away from home for the first time, he gravitated into the company of the riff-raff of Liverpool, and was soon drinking and gambling heavily. Inevitably his salary as a pharmaceutical apprentice was meagre and his mother helped him out financially. Even so this was insufficient to pay his debts, and he began to appropriate money sent to the company in payment of accounts. He was eventually caught in the act, and his apprenticeship abruptly terminated.

Mrs Palmer, who refused to believe anything bad about her 'darling Billy', cast around for alternative employment and managed to obtain a post for him as a student with a Dr Edward Tylecote at Haywood, in Cheshire. William showed an aptitude for medicine, particularly in the study of vegetable poisons, a subject which, at the time, was claiming the attention of many researchers. But though he was interested in his work he was even more interested in the opposite sex. Dr Tylecote started receiving complaints about Palmer's excessive familiarity towards female patients and once again Palmer found his contract terminated.

With a record such as this behind him, it says much for Mrs Palmer's determination that in 1842 she succeeded in getting William registered as a medical student at the Stafford Infirmary. Here he worked hard, though again he quickly acquired a reputation for drinking and gambling. This, however, did not stop him from doing well in his medical studies, and in 1846 he travelled to London and took his qualifying examination at St Bartholomew's Hospital. His return to Rugeley as a qualified physician was marred only by the curious episode of the death of Walter Abley, a farmer with whom Palmer was friendly. He was even more friendly with Mrs Abley, and when her husband dropped dead after a brandy-drinking contest with Palmer there were unkind rumours that the newly-qualified doctor had precipitated the death. Palmer was called as a witness at the inquest, but nothing could be proved against him. The death of Mr Abley remained a mystery but Palmer ceased paying attention to the widow immediately afterwards.

He was at the time a fine-looking young man, immensely popular with the ladies. His popularity may be gauged by the fact that during his four years at Stafford he fathered no less than fifteen illegitimate children and was strongly suspected of having organized the abortions of many more.

His father had died some years before leaving £75,000. William's share was £9,000 which he inherited when he was twenty-one, the year before he qualified. At the age of twenty-three Palmer decided that the attractions and rewards of the racecourse were far greater than those of medicine. He spent most of his days at the races and neglected his medical practice in the town, though, curiously enough, he always left himself time to administer to the poor and needy.

Though by now a confirmed gambler, Palmer did not have much success on the turf and his capital began to dwindle rapidly. He looked around for another source of income and found it in the form of a young lady called Annie Thornton. She was the illegitimate daughter of the notoriously eccentric Rugeley man, Colonel Edward Brookes, and his housekeeper Mary Thornton, whom he refused to marry. Annie was a ward in Chancery, and one of her guardians was Dr Tylecote, to whom Palmer had been apprenticed and in whose house the two had first met. She had inherited £8,000 and Dr Tylecote, well aware of Palmer's character and the reason for his interest in Annie, strenuously opposed the development of any friendship between them.

Palmer was, however, ardent in his wooing, and Annie fell deeply in love with him. The two young people were determined to have their way, and eventually obtained a court order in their favour. Palmer and Annie were married at Rugeley in August 1847. While Annie must have been aware of the sort of man she was marrying, she was probably innocent enough to believe that he would now settle down and that her influence would result in him becoming a model husband and father. Like many another girl who believed she could change her husband after marriage, she was disappointed. Palmer continued gambling, using her money when his was at an end, and still pursuing women.

A year after the marriage one of the housemaids had a child by Palmer. Surprisingly enough, Annie (herself pregnant by then) forgave her husband and even made arrangements for the baby boy to be looked after by a foster-mother. Because of the cost, Palmer would not agree to this course at first, but later he relented and a suitable foster-mother was found. A few months later, when the baby was brought to Palmer's house for his father to see, he took it into the dispensary for a few minutes. The child went into convulsions immediately, and was dead in a very short time. Palmer expressed the greatest sorrow, but there was no doubt that the death of the child relieved him of a worrying financial responsibility.

By 1848 Palmer had not only dissipated his own fortune of £9,000 but also most of the £8,000 inherited through his wife. His mother, long convinced that her son could do nothing wrong and was the victim of bad luck, had helped him through many crises ever since his days at Liverpool. But now she suddenly decided that enough was enough and informed her offspring that he could expect no further monies from her. This was a serious blow to Palmer, and once more he found himself looking round for a likely source of income.

That he was getting near the bottom of the financial barrel is indicated by the fact that one of the very few people left to whom he could turn was his mother-in-law, Mary Thornton. Unfortunately she had never approved of Palmer and, with Dr Tylecote, had strenuously opposed the marriage. But such was the persuasiveness of her son-in-law that not only did she agree to lend him small sums, but in 1849 she also came to live with the Palmers as a paying guest. Her stay did not last long. Within a few weeks she began to suffer from acute bouts of biliousness which Palmer, apparently, was unable to alleviate. He called in a Dr Bamford, an eighty-year-old semi-retired practitioner who lived locally, but he too could do little for the stricken woman. Dr Bamford was conscious of his declining powers as a physician, and repeatedly suggested to Palmer that he should send for Dr Knight, Mary Thornton's own doctor, but this he declined to do.

Dr Bamford continued prescribing alkaline effervescent mixtures, which Palmer made up in his own dispensary, but Mrs Thornton became more and more ill. She finally died in great agony, but not before raising herself on one arm in bed, pointing at Palmer and shouting, 'Take that devil away from me!' By this time she must have suspected her son-in-law of poisoning her, but it was too late. Dr Bamford, after consulting with Palmer, signed a certificate giving the cause of death as acute apoplexy. When, at the funeral, Dr Knight asked Palmer why he had not been sent for, in view of his patient's condition, Palmer blandly replied that Mrs Thornton had not wished him to call.

Mary Thornton left £12,000 in her will, but much to Palmer's chagrin the money was in trust and Annie could draw on the interest only. His affairs were in a parlous state. He owed considerable sums of money all round, he was barred from Tattersalls for the non-payment of a debt, and found it difficult to find a bookmaker who would do business with him.

He was, however, still friendly with many men who frequented the racecourse and, despite his reputation, some of them retained their confidence in him. One was a director of the local brewery, Leonard Bladon, who had often gambled with Palmer. In 1850 Palmer owed Bladon £600 but could not pay him.

It so happened that Palmer and Bladon were together at the Chester racecourse when Bladon won £500, drawing his winnings in cash. Palmer suggested that he was now in a position to repay Bladon and would do so if the brewer would come to his house and stay a day or two while he collected the necessary cash. Bladon, pleased with what he saw as a double stroke of good fortune, readily agreed, but first sent a message to his wife advising her of the situation and saying he would not be home for a day or two.

Once at Palmer's house the unfortunate Bladon began to suffer from severe bouts of indigestion. Inevitably the attacks got worse, and Bladon had to go to bed. Palmer attended to him, giving him draughts to alleviate his condition, but once again, there was no improvement. The aged Dr Bamford was called in but had no more success than he had had with Mary Thornton. At that point, by chance, a friend of Bladon happened to call at Palmer's house and was shocked to see his friend so ill. He asked Palmer if Mrs Bladon had been notified, but Palmer said it was quite unnecessary as Bladon would be home again within a few days. The man was far from satisfied and hurried to Mrs Bladon to advise her of her husband's condition. She in turn went to Palmer's house, only to be told by Palmer that her husband was very seriously ill and that his life was despaired of. An hour after she arrived, her husband died.

Mrs Bladon was grief-stricken, but after a few days recovered sufficiently to enquire about the £500 her husband had told her he had won at the races. Alas, said Palmer, he had no personal knowledge of this matter. This was despite the fact that a mutual friend declared that Bladon had actually shown him the £500 in his money-belt the very day he had gone to Palmer's house. What, then, persisted Mrs Bladon, of the £600 Palmer owed to her husband. The doctor was even more reluctant to break the sad news. He did not owe any money to Bladon, he said. On the contrary Bladon owed *him* £60 which, as he was rather short at the moment, he would be obliged if Mrs Bladon would settle as soon as possible.

At her wit's end, Mrs Bladon called a family conference. Her brother-in-law, a shoemaker in Leicestershire, was highly suspicious of Palmer, particularly in view of the speed with which Palmer had arranged Bladon's burial. The family wanted Mrs Bladon to go to the police, but this she refused to do. She could not really believe that the doctor was the villain her family thought he was, and in any case investigation of the matter would have involved her in further expense. She decided to cut her losses and let the matter drop, though she refused to pay Palmer the £60.

A rather similar situation occurred when a man named Blyth, to whom Palmer owed £800, fell ill and died. Though the death could not in any way be attributed to Palmer, when the sorrowing widow approached the doctor for re-payment of the loan he told her that she had been mis-informed. He owed her husband nothing, he said. On the contrary, Blyth owed *him* £800! After some discussion Palmer graciously informed Mrs Blyth that he did not intend to press for payment.

In 1852, despite his growing monetary problems, Palmer acquired a small racing-stable near Rugeley. His assets were almost nil, and in order to finance this new venture he had to resort to money-lenders; but even these required some sort of security, and to provide this Palmer took to forging his mother's signature on various forms guaranteeing repayment. Old Mrs Palmer was well known in Rugeley as 'a character' — and a very wealthy 'character' at that — and her signature on the forms was accepted without question.

The money-lenders concerned in this transaction were two unscrupulous rogues named Padwick and Pratt, who lent money at exorbitant rates of interest. It was essential that they did not contact the old lady on the matter of the guarantees, or the forgeries would have come to light. In the 1850s forgery for financial gain was still an offence punishable by transportation for life, and this was something the doctor had no intention of risking. He therefore arranged with Samuel Cheshire, the Rugeley postmaster, and a friend, that all mail for his mother should be diverted to him before delivery. For this grossly unethical and illegal conduct Cheshire himself was later to be sentenced to twelve months' hard labour.

But for the moment this plot got Palmer out of his difficulties though, as he well knew, the loans would eventually have to be repaid. Only a very large win at the races could save him, and this was what Palmer was relying upon.

In his private life he seemed a reasonably satisfactory husband. Annie turned a blind eye to his heavy drinking and his frequent absences at the racecourse. He attended church regularly with his wife. Between 1848 and 1854 the couple had five children, but only the eldest survived, the others dying in infancy. Later there were those who said that their father, while dandling them on his knee, had murdered them one by one with poisoned jam, but the rate of infant mortality was so high in early Victorian times that the deaths of these small children may not have been all that surprising. Even so, four infant deaths out of five was certainly a large proportion, even for those days. It is possible that Palmer was experimenting with different poisons during this period.

There was about this time the odd incident of Palmer's uncle, a near-alcoholic known locally as 'Beau' Bentley, who came to stay with the Palmers. Like the unfortunate Walter Abley he too was challenged by Palmer to a brandy-drinking contest. He won, but died a few hours afterwards. Again, an aunt who visited the Palmers for a short holiday was taken ill with violent stomach-ache immediately after arriving. She was given some pills by Palmer but, for some reason best known to herself, was unwilling to take them. Instead, she threw them out of the bedroom window, where they landed in a chicken-run. The next morning half the hens were dead and Palmer was most insistent that none of the birds should be eaten by the family.

If the death of the uncle was murder and the episode of the pills attempted murder, there is no logical reason for this, as neither of these relatives had any money. It might well have been an attempt by Palmer to evaluate the potency of various poisonous substances in preparation for more worthwhile experiments.

It seems certain that about this time the doctor began to examine the possibilities of financial gain by way of insurance. The subject was to be his own wife, Annie. He had a word with a close friend, Jeremiah Smith, an un-scrupulous solicitor who was also the Rugeley agent for the Prince of Wales Insurance Company. With Smith's con-nivance he insured Annie's life for £13,000 at a premium of £760 a year. Without the help of the solicitor the company would surely have queried the insurance on the life of such a healthy young woman for so large a sum. Proper investiga-tion of Palmer's affairs would also have revealed that he had insufficient funds to pay the premium. Palmer managed to borrow the money, possibly from Smith himself; at all events the first premium was paid in March 1854.

In September of that year Annie Palmer, accompanied by a relative, went to Liverpool for a short stay with friends.

She caught a severe chill soon after arriving, and after only three days away returned home to Rugeley. She took to her bed, and her husband assumed the reponsibility of looking after her, cooking all her food and preparing her medicine. Her condition worsened steadily and she began complaining of cramps in her muscles and abdomen, while suffering from sickness and diarrhoea. Once again Palmer called in Dr Bamford, and once again the aged doctor suggested consulting Dr Knight from Stafford. This time Palmer readily agreed. Dr Knight's immediate diagnosis was that Annie was in the first stage of an attack of cholera, the dread disease that had first spread to Europe from India in 1831 and had been claiming more victims in a fresh epidemic which began in 1847. Put on a starvation diet by Knight the patient began to improve, and after two days Dr Knight went home, arranging that Palmer would send for him should Annie deteriorate.

A few days later she suddenly did become worse and Dr Knight was summoned once more. Unfortunately he arrived too late, and Annie died just before he reached the house. After consulting with Palmer and Bamford, Knight issued a certificate showing the cause of death as English cholera.

Palmer made a great show of being heart-broken, and recorded in his diary, 'Saw the last of my beloved wife for ever. How desolate life is!' He also remarked to a friend, 'I shall not be long before I follow her.' In view of the fact that the later exhumation of Annie's body proved she had been murdered by the ingestion of large quantities of antimony, it is a pity, in a way, that Palmer did not have a bet on this. It would have been one of his more successful forecasts!

In the meantime the insurance company, though a little suspicious, had no grounds for withholding payment and Palmer received his £13,000. With this he was able to repay £8,000 of the loan from Pratt and Padwick and settle other debts amounting to £5,000.

Palmer was pleased with himself. The scheme had worked well, and he had only to find another suitable candidate to bring it off again. The victim presented himself in the form of Palmer's elder brother, Walter, a retired corn-merchant much addicted to the bottle. Incredible as it may seem, though Palmer was refused by two other insurance companies the Prince of Wales agreed to insure Walter's life for £14,000 despite two independent doctors reporting that he was a near-alcoholic.

Palmer then arranged for Walter, who lived apart from his wife Agnes, to be looked after by a bibulous couple named Walkenden, who were told by the doctor to ensure that Walter was never short of a drink. The only slight difficulty about the scheme was that under normal circumstances, if anything happened to Walter, the insurance money would be payable to his wife. Palmer got over this problem by persuading Walter to sign over the insurance to him on the promise of an immediate payment of £400.

Walter lived in Stafford, and when Palmer went to see him he put up for the night at the Grand Junction hotel. Before visiting his brother, Palmer bought some prussic acid from a chemist in Wolverhampton, and was later seen by the Boots at the hotel mixing the contents of a small, green bottle into a normal-sized bottle of medicine. The doctor explained to the lad that as he was away from his dispensary he had to make up his brother's medicine on the premises. Palmer visited the sick man that afternoon. The morning after, Walter was dead.

Agnes Palmer did not even know her husband was ill, though she guessed that alcoholism might one day kill him. On hearing of his death she hurried to the house and found that her husband was already buried, a fact which annoyed her intensely. Nor was she aware, until told by Palmer, that he had insured her husband's life and that the benefits had been transferred to him. Agnes Palmer was livid with rage, especially when Palmer informed her that Walter had also owed him a considerable sum of money. She returned home in a highly distraught state, and vowed she would not pay Palmer a penny.

Though Walter's death had been independently certified by another doctor as due to apoplexy caused by excess alcohol, the insurance company refused to pay and treated the whole affair with the utmost suspicion. They defied Palmer to take them to court – something which the doctor, perhaps understandably, was not willing to do.

The outlook for Palmer was bleak indeed, with both Pratt and Padwick pressing for the balance of the loans ostensibly guaranteed by Palmer's mother. In the absence of a large win at the races, Palmer had only one course of action. He had to find another victim whose life he could insure for an even larger sum.

He therefore approached the Globe Insurance Company with a proposal to insure the life of 'a gentleman of leisure with substantial holdings' for the sum of £25,000. In the event the 'gentleman of leisure' proved to be a mentally-retarded youth known as George Bates, employed by Palmer as a stable-lad at £1 a week. Bates was persuaded to sign the application form on the understanding that for this service he would receive £500 immediately.

On receipt of the proposal the Globe sent two insurance officers to Rugeley to investigate the application. They found Bates mucking out the stables and it soon became apparent that he was a mental deficient and that the whole affair was highly suspect. They confronted Palmer and virtually accused him of having engineered the deaths of his wife and brother. Palmer said loftily that if suspicion was attached to their deaths there must be a poisoner at large in the district, but that he had no knowledge of the matter.

Palmer was now in a critical situation. Not only were

Padwick and Pratt threatening to issue writs against Mrs Palmer, but Palmer was also being blackmailed by a woman named Jane Burgess who had in her possession some incriminating letters in which he described the arrangements being made for her to procure an abortion.

It was with this background that Palmer attended Shrewsbury races in November 1855 with a friend called John Parsons Cook, a wild young man who was a horse-trainer and a heavy, but usually lucky, gambler.

Desperate, Palmer risked all in a last throw and lost his money. Cook, on the other hand, was more fortunate and won over £2,000 on his own horse, Polestar, taking about £800 of his winnings in cash. The balance was to be paid the following week by Tattersalls in London. From that moment on the life of John Parsons Cook was in jeopardy, for Palmer there and then decided to kill his friend and avail himself of the winnings. That evening there was a celebration party at the Shrewsbury hotel at which Palmer, Cook and others of the racing fraternity were staying. During the evening Cook was taken ill. He accused Palmer of doping his drink and gave all his money into the custody of a close friend, Ishmael Fisher.

He was so ill during the night that a doctor was called, and Cook openly expressed the fear that he was being poisoned. Accordingly the doctor gave him an emetic, which seemed to relieve his distress. As regards the accusation of poisoning, Palmer told the doctor that Cook had been drunk when he expressed that opinion and that there was nothing to it. Later, witnesses were to swear that Cook had had only three glasses of wine during the evening for, unlike most of his racing friends, he was a very abstemious man.

The next morning Cook, though still feeling somewhat weak, insisted on attending the races, again in the company of Palmer. There he met Ishmael Fisher who handed back the money he had been keeping for him from the night before. Palmer had one of his own horses, The Chicken, running in the 3.30 race and backed it to win £5,000. It was unplaced.

During the day Cook seems to have overcome his suspicions of Palmer, for when the meeting was over he readily agreed to return with the doctor to Rugeley. He put up at the Talbot Arms, a well-known hotel immediately opposite Palmer's house, where he had often stayed before.

That night Palmer gave a dinner party for his friends which Cook attended, returning to the hotel well after midnight. He was seen by the porter who was later to say that he appeared perfectly sober.

The following morning Palmer arrived very early at the hotel, and asked for a cup of black coffee to take up to Cook. His friend, he said, was sure to be suffering from a violent hangover due to his excessive drinking the night before. As soon as he had drunk the coffee Cook became extremely sick and complained of severe abdominal pains. He was ill on and off for the rest of the day, Palmer ferrying endless cups of coffee up and down stairs and at one point taking his friend a bowl of soup which, oddly enough, he had procured from another hotel near the Talbot Arms. Cook did not finish the soup and the remains were taken down to the kitchen. There a maid, thinking how appetizing it looked, took several spoonfuls. She was immediately stricken with severe stomach cramps and took five hours to recover.

During the day Palmer once again called in old Dr Bamford who was willing to agree with Palmer (as he was willing to agree with anything Palmer said) that Cook's illness was caused by too much drink the night before. Later that evening Palmer was seen in a corridor of the hotel holding up a tumbler to the light and vigorously stirring the contents. He then took it into Cook's room and within minutes the wretched man was seized with a fresh bout of stomach pain accompanied by violent retching. However,

21

he was still alive the next morning, no doubt much to Palmer's surprise.

Palmer had a very busy time ahead of him the next day and was up early to catch a train to London. On arrival, the first thing he did was to visit Tattersalls. He explained to the clerk that Cook was ill, and that he had been authorized to collect the £1,200 due to him. Though Palmer himself was barred from doing business with Tattersalls, the clerk took his word for it and handed over the money. Palmer then paid off his own debt to Tattersalls, and asked the clerk to remit various monies direct to Pratt and Padwick, giving the impression that they were debts that Cook owed these men. In reality, of course, they were part of his own indebtedness to the money-lenders.

From this moment onwards it became essential to Palmer that Cook should not go on living, for if he survived the misappropriation of his winnings would come to light, Pratt and Padwick would serve their writs on Mrs Palmer, and the doctor would be revealed as an embezzler and forger. He was forced to act speedily.

On arriving back in Rugeley from London he had several other calls to make before he reached home. His first action was to call on a Dr Newton, recently arrived in the town, and borrow three grains of strychnine hydrochloride on the pretext that it was needed urgently for a patient and he was out of stock. Doctors, like pharmacists, are accustomed to helping each other out with supplies of various medicaments, and Newton thought nothing of it. Nor was the request for strychnine particularly sinister as at that period a minute dose of the drug, together with potassium bromide, was very popular as a tonic. In fact it has much to commend it, and appears in the *British Pharmacopoeia* to this day.

Palmer then went to his friend Cheshire, the postmaster, and asked him to fill in one of Cook's own cheque forms, as Cook himself was too ill to do this. The cheque was to be for

£350, payable to Palmer, and Cheshire filled it in with some reluctance. The signature was left blank, and Palmer later forged Cook's name on it. When Cheshire asked Palmer why he could not fill in the cheque himself, Palmer gave the curious answer that he was afraid the bank might recognize his handwriting.

When Palmer eventually arrived home he went into his dispensary and quickly made up the strychnine into a batch of pills.

The next morning Palmer sought out Dr Bamford and told him that Cook had had a very bad night but was recovered enough to have a little breakfast. He asked the aged doctor to prescribe some ammonia pills, these being a favourite form of stomach sedative in Victorian times. Palmer then insisted that Bamford should write the directions on the label of the box in his own hand, despite the fact that both doctors knew perfectly well how the pills should be taken.

During that day Palmer also sent the following message to Lutterworth to summon Cook's own physician, a Dr William Jones:

Rugeley, 18th November 1855
My Dear Sir,
Mr Cook was taken ill at Shrewsbury and obliged to call in a medical man; since then he has been confined to his bed here with a very severe bilious attack, combined with diarrhoea, and I think it advisable for you to come and see him as soon as possible.
Yours faithfully,
William Palmer.

This was written by Palmer on the Sunday, and received by Dr Jones the following day. Unfortunately Jones himself was ill on Monday and unable to travel to Rugeley, but he did so the next day, arriving about 3.30 in the afternoon. He booked in at the Talbot Arms and immediately went to see his patient. Palmer was there, and the first thing Jones noticed when he examined Cook was that the sick man's pulse was normal and his tongue uncoated. There was no sign of biliousness or diarrhoea, and Jones decided that whatever was wrong with his patient it was something rather different from a normal stomach upset.

Later that evening Cook was persuaded to take some pills, and Palmer went across to his house to get them. On his return he took good care to show the box to Jones, remarking as he did so, 'What an excellent hand for an old man of eighty to write.' The reason for this was probably to impress upon Jones the fact that Cook had been under the care of Bamford throughout his illness.

As it was approaching midnight, Dr Jones prepared to spend the night in Cook's room and Palmer returned to his own house. Only ten minutes later Cook went into convulsions and Dr Jones sent a maid across the road to fetch Palmer. He arrived fully dressed within minutes — he had probably been waiting for the call, though he remarked to Jones, 'I never dressed so quickly in all my life.'

Palmer noticed that Jones was massaging Cook's neck, and when he asked about this Jones told him that Cook had been complaining that all his muscles, but particularly his neck muscles, had been becoming progressively more rigid. Palmer wanted Cook to be given more pills, but by then the man's jaws were clenched and his limbs beginning to stiffen. Cook died a few minutes after midnight in terrible agony, his body arched like a bow and supported only by his head and his heels.

Dr Jones immediately went downstairs to advise the hotel proprietor of the death, and a maid, peeping into the room, was just in time to see Palmer searching the dead man's clothing and looking under the mattress. When Jones returned Palmer handed him Cook's coat, together with five gold sovereigns and a watch, saying that these seemed to be Cook's entire possessions. He also told Jones that Cook owed him £4,000 and added, 'It is a bad thing for me, and I hope Mr Cook's friends will not let me lose it. If they do not assist me all my horses will be seized.'

The next day Palmer called on his old friend, Samuel Cheshire, and showed him a document supposedly signed by Cook admitting a debt of £4,000 to Palmer. He asked Cheshire to witness Cook's signature, but Cheshire, though he had obliged Palmer so often in the past, refused to do so this time on the grounds that Cook was dead. 'No matter,' said Palmer cheerfully, 'I have no doubt the signature will be accepted.'

In the meantime Dr Jones had got in touch with Cook's nearest known relative, his stepfather, William Stevens, a retired merchant who lived in London and a man noted for his surliness and bad temper. Stevens arrived at Rugeley on the Thursday, viewed the body, and asked Palmer if he had any knowledge of his stepson's financial affairs. 'Indeed I have,' said Palmer, 'He owes me £4,000.'

Stevens took an instant dislike to Palmer, whom he thought callous and grasping, and expressed great surprise that his stepson should owe money to anybody. His temper was not improved when he discovered that Palmer had already been to the undertaker and not only chosen a coffin but also arranged for the funeral service. He told Palmer in no uncertain terms that he had no authority to do this, particularly as Cook had always expressed the wish to be buried in the family vault in London. Palmer shrugged, saying he had only done his best.

Later that evening, when Stevens invited Bamford and Jones to dine with him he found Palmer with them, and, much against his will, extended the invitation to him. During the course of the evening Stevens enquired about Cook's betting-book which, with papers, had been seen by both Jones and Bamford on the mantelpiece in Cook's bedroom. Jones volunteered to go upstairs and fetch them, but returned a few minutes later to report that both book and papers had vanished. Stevens was very annoyed at this, but Palmer dismissed the matter with his usual airiness, saying 'Oh, I dare say it will turn up sooner or later.' The following day Palmer asked Dr Bamford to provide a death certificate for Cook. This rather surprised the old man, who said that he was under the impression that Palmer had been looking after him. But Palmer was at his most persuasive, and Bamford dutifully wrote the certificate showing death due to apoplexy – evidently Bamford's favourite diagnosis.

At the week-end Stevens returned to London for a day or two. Palmer also decided to pay a visit to the capital, to pay off more debts, and the two men happened to meet at Euston Station on the return journey. The train was crowded, and though they were both in the same compartment conversation was impossible until they reached Rugeley. When they alighted Stevens told Palmer that he was suspicious of the circumstances surrounding Cook's death, and was going to demand a post-mortem. He also said that he was seeing a solicitor in an attempt to discover more details of his stepson's financial affairs.

Stevens stayed again at the Talbot Arms, and for the next few days Palmer dogged his steps. He appeared in the coffee-room, in the bar, or in the dining-room whenever Stevens was present, rarely speaking to him but watching him closely and attempting to overhear his conversations with others.

The post-mortem was finally fixed for Monday 26th November. It was to take place at the Talbot Arms, in a small room set aside by the management, and was to be conducted by two local practitioners, Dr John Harland and Dr George Newton. Palmer knew them both. First he sought out Harland and said to him, 'You must be on your guard. There is a very queer old man beating up this matter. He suspects me of something and seems to think I have Cook's betting-book.'

Palmer's approach to Newton, a much younger man, was rather different. Immediately before the post-mortem was due to start he suddenly began offering him brandy, no doubt in an effort to get him intoxicated. But Newton refused all offers of alcohol.

Although Palmer was the first to insist that it was Bamford and not himself who had attended the dead man, he cheerfully invited himself to the autopsy 'as Cook's best friend' and appeared to treat the whole thing as rather a joke. In the small room provided by the hotel were, in addition to the corpse, Harland, Newton, Jones, Bamford and Palmer, and it must have been under some difficulty that Harland and Newton carried out their examination, removing various organs from the body. At one point Harland was about to put the stomach and the intestines into a glass jar, but just as he was doing so he received a sudden push in the back from Palmer, and nearly dropped the material on the floor. Palmer looked round, pretending to see who had jostled him, but as he had his back to a wall, this display was scarcely convincing. A few minutes later Newton, preparing to put another specimen into the jar, found the jar was not on the table. Palmer had it in his hands and was about to leave the room. When asked what he was doing he said that as there was so little space available he was putting it into a safer place for the time being.

It is obvious that Palmer was trying to destroy the evidence, or at the very least make it unsuitable for expert examination. This is proved by his later action, when he discovered that the glass jars containing the remains were being taken to London for examination by the Home Office pathologist, Dr Swaine Taylor. Enquiries revealed that the jars were to be taken by fly from Rugeley to Stafford station, to be put on the London train. Palmer went to the post-boy in charge of the fly and said to him, 'They have no right to take those jars to London; one does not know what they may have put in them. Can't you manage to upset the fly and break them? I will give you £10 and make things all right for you.' The post-boy indignantly refused to be party to this scheme, and later told Dr Newton what Palmer had suggested.

While Palmer was waiting for the result of the examination of the remains by Professor Taylor, he kept busy by ingratiating himself with the coroner who was to conduct the inquest. Though he scarcely knew the man, he sent him a brace of pheasant, a turkey and a barrel of oysters. The views of the coroner on these sudden and unexpected gifts is not recorded. Because of his peculiar conduct, those acquainted with the circumstances surrounding the death of Cook became increasingly suspicious of the doctor. It was openly suggested that Palmer had poisoned Cook, and this, and his financial wheeling and dealing, became the talk of the town.

The outcome of Dr Swaine Taylor's examination was awaited in a fever of excitement. When the pathologist finally wrote to Dr Newton it was to tell him that Cook had certainly not died from natural causes, but probably from a poison akin to strychnine, on which Taylor himself was a known authority. However he had been unable to find any strychnine in the body, though he had found antimony to be present.

One of the most interested in Dr Taylor's findings was, of course, Palmer himself. With the help of Samuel Cheshire he arranged for Taylor's letter to Newton to be intercepted. On reading it, Palmer wrote once more to the coroner, gleefully telling him that he had private information that Dr Taylor had found no strychnine in Cook's body. Accompanying this letter was another brace of pheasant!

The inquest was held at Rugeley on 18th December, and there Dr Taylor gave evidence of his examination of Cook's remains and reiterated the facts contained in his letter.

By this time Pratt and Padwick, having given up any hope of having their debts settled, had issued writs against old Mrs Palmer and the whole affair of the forgeries and false pretences had come to light. When the inquest jury, after only a short retirement, brought in a verdict of murder, Palmer was already lodged in Stafford Gaol. Once the verdict was known the authorities quickly exhumed the bodies of Palmer's wife and that of his brother, Walter. Large quantities of antimony and some arsenic were found in each, and a tide of fury rose against the doctor. It was fortunate, for his own safety, that he was protected by the walls of the prison.

Such was the degree of local feeling against Palmer that it was decided that it would be impossible to empanel a jury which was not already prejudiced against him. At that time there was no provision for trying a criminal other than in the county where his offence was committed. An Act was therefore rushed through Parliament, known to this day as Palmer's Act, which removed this prohibition and as a result arrangements were made for Palmer to stand trial at the Old Bailey, the Central Criminal Court in London.

The trial began on Wednesday 14th May, 1856, before Lord Chief Justice Campbell sitting with two other judges. The prosecution was in the hands of Sir Alexander Cockburn, the Attorney-General, and Palmer was defended by the eminent advocate, Serjeant Shee. The trial took twelve days and was remarkable for the number of witnesses — sixty-six for the prosecution and twenty-three for the defence.

The outlining of the case for the prosecution was something of a *tour de force* by the Attorney-General, lasting the whole of the first day and amounting to some 40,000 words.

29

It sketched the backgrounds and life-styles of both Cook and Palmer and was a model of its kind in its clarity and in the way it described Palmer's complicated financial dealings, which provided a motive for the murder.

In the days that followed witness after witness came to the box to provide testimony of Palmer's suspicious behaviour on many occasions and included the important evidence of Drs Harland, Newton and Bamford. One of the prosecution's difficulties was that little was known of the action of strychnine except that it produced tetanic convulsions similar to those of lockjaw — a fact eagerly seized upon by Serjeant Shee for the defence. According to him Cook could easily have died of tetanus poisoning brought about by the infection of some small and scarcely-noticed wound. Another line of defence was that Cook thought he was suffering from syphilis and had been dosing himself with mercury. Unfortunately there was evidence that he had stopped doing this several months before his death. Yet again the defence suggested that he was, in reality, an epileptic, and it was seizure due to this disease that had caused his death.

Many eminent surgeons and physicians gave evidence on both sides, the prosecution relying to a great extent on the evidence of the famous pathologist and toxicologist Dr Swaine Taylor and that of his colleague, Sir Benjamin Brodie, surgeon to Queen Victoria. Lined up for the defence were Thomas Nunnely, Professor of Surgery at Leeds School of Medicine, William Herepath, Professor of Toxicology at Bristol Medical School and John Brown Ross, surgeon at the London Hospital. All of them described in detail deaths they had witnessed brought about by tetanus poisoning in an attempt to persuade the jury that this was the cause of Cook's death. But Taylor and Brodie between them showed conclusively that tetanus was a disease caused by an infection, absent in Cook's case, and that the 'tetanic convulsions' had been brought about by the introduction of a poison, or possibly several poisons, at different times.

At last it was the turn of the presiding judge to sum up for the jury, a process which took another full day. Considering the length of the trial and the mass of complicated evidence which had been heard, the jury were not out for long. In just over an hour, on 27th May, they returned a verdict of guilty against Palmer. The three judges agreed that the verdict was 'eminently suitable' and the Lord Chief Justice pronounced the sentence of death.

Palmer's comment, when the verdict was returned, was that he was 'not guilty of poisoning Cook with strychnine'. It was a curious statement, neither a confession nor an admission, but there is certainly little doubt that he succeeded in killing Cook with some poison or other. Palmer also commented on the result of his trial that 'it was the riding that did it', by which, in racecourse language, he meant that it was the professional expertise and advocacy of the Attorney-General that had won the day. He said that all along he had been hoping for an acquittal. 'But,' he added, 'when the jury returned into Court, and I saw the cocked-up nose of that perky little foreman, I knew I was a goner!'

Palmer was hanged outside Stafford Gaol at eight o'clock on the morning of 14th June 1856 before an enormous crowd. A contemporary account describes his last moments on earth:

> On the morning of the execution the path from the condemned cell to the gallows was wet and muddy, it having rained during the night, and Palmer minced along like a delicate schoolgirl, picking his way and avoiding the puddles. He was particularly anxious not to get his feet wet. He was received on the scaffold with a deafening round of curses, shouts, oaths and execrations from a crowd of between twenty and thirty thousand people. Palmer cast just one look on the vast multitude around

31

him, and shook hands with the executioner, to whom he said 'God bless you'. The drop immediately fell, and the greatest of criminals died without a struggle.

Whether or not he was 'the greatest' of criminals is debatable, but it is thought that he certainly murdered twelve people, and may have been responsible for many more deaths.

Old Mrs Palmer, when acquainted of the news of her son's execution, voiced the memorable phrase, 'They've hanged my saintly Billy'. Equally memorable was the quip of the Prime Minister of the day when the good people of Rugeley petitioned Parliament to have the name of the town changed, in view of the notoriety of the case. 'Certainly,' said he, 'why don't they name it after me?' The Prime Minister was Palmerston.

2

Thomas Smethurst

(1805-?)

Whether or not the genial Dr Thomas Smethurst was really guilty of murder in 1859 will always remain a profound mystery. Certainly there was plenty of evidence produced on both sides, for no less than ten doctors were called for the prosecution whilst seven equally well-qualified practitioners gave contrary evidence for the defence. If anything at all was proved by the Smethurst case it was that medical experts rarely agree, even on comparatively simple matters. Those of us who have occasion to study the medical press are constantly surprised at the divergence of opinion displayed by experienced doctors on subjects which the layman thinks were settled years ago.

The result of this is that an individual accused of murder by poisoning has a good chance of acquittal if the evidence is purely medical. It requires much more than this to convict a poisoner, as was shown in the final result of this famous trial. In addition to the amount of contrary evidence adduced, there was the astonishing mistake made by Dr Swaine Taylor, the most 'expert' witness of all, and a leading figure in the William Palmer trial three years earlier. Though the judge, in his summing-up, took the view that one mistake by an expert did not invalidate the remainder of his evidence, there were many who felt uneasy about the first verdict which ended the trial.

It is possible that the jury were influenced less by the medical evidence than by the moral issues involved – the fact that the doctor had 'seduced' an innocent spinster, deserted his wife and bigamously married his victim. What is undoubtedly true is that today, over a hundred years later, with the same evidence available against Smethurst he would never come to trial.

The Smethursts lived in Bayswater, a part of London still noted for its small hotels and cheap boarding-houses, and an area with a constantly shifting population where no questions are asked as long as the rent is paid regularly. It was so even in 1858 when Dr Thomas Smethurst and his wife, Mary, took lodgings in the boarding-house run by Mrs Smith at No. 4 Rifle Terrace.

The doctor was a short, plump little man with a heavy walrus moustache and side-whiskers, exceedingly friendly and genial. Mrs Smith was pleased to have a medical man as a lodger, but noted with some surprise how very much older than her husband Mrs Smethurst was. In fact the doctor was fifty-three years old in 1858 while his wife was well into her seventies, though this disparity in age did not seem to minimise the very real affection which each displayed towards the other.

Mrs Smith, as an experienced Bayswater landlady, did not ask many questions but was able to piece together the information that the couple had been married thirty years, and that the doctor had travelled extensively in Europe, particularly Germany. There he had studied the cult of hydrotherapy, the system which maintains that most ailments can eventually be cured by the application of ice-cold douches in the most unlikely places. He had also run an establishment of his own on these lines at Farnham, in Surrey, and had written a book on the subject.

The Smethursts arrived at Rifle Terrace in April 1858 and settled in quite happily, finding it both convenient for the shops in Westbourne Grove and for the brighter lights of the West End. It was also handy for the semi-rural ambience of Hyde Park and Kensington Gardens.

Towards the end of September that year Rifle Terrace acquired a new lodger, Miss Isabella Bankes, a spinster of forty-two. Frail and anaemic-looking, she was still possessed of a delicate charm though subject to bouts of biliousness. She was also said to be very wealthy.

One of the occupational hazards of the medical profession is that many people, after even a short acquaintance with a doctor, have a yearning to launch into a description of their most intimate symptoms. Miss Bankes was no exception and had a wealth of material at her disposal. Before long she was describing to Dr Smethurst the detailed workings of her digestive organs, and it was inevitable that he should give her advice.

Very soon he was attending her in her room and Mrs Smith became concerned about the length of time these consultations were taking, usually behind locked doors. She discussed the matter with her husband, but he was more concerned that the rent was paid regularly every fortnight, and in advance. Mrs Smith continued to worry, however, and her fears of a scandal within the respectable doors of her establishment were compounded when friends and neighbours reported seeing Miss Bankes and the doctor walking arm-in-arm in the gloaming in Kensington Gardens, obviously on very good terms. Mrs Smethurst appeared to be unconcerned with these events and the loving relationship between her and her husband apparently continued as before.

Despite this, Mrs Smith decided to act. She told Miss Bankes that she did not approve of the growing familiarity between her and the doctor, and asked her to leave. With very little fuss, Miss Bankes packed her bag and, on 29th November, moved round the corner into new lodgings in Kildare Terrace. Dr Smethurst seemed very contrite about the affair, and assured Mrs Smith that he would rather move himself than cause Miss Bankes any inconvenience. But it was too late, and Miss Bankes had already gone.

Ten days later Dr Smethurst also vanished from Rifle Terrace, leaving his wife behind. Though Mrs Smith was not aware of it, on 9th December he had joined Miss Bankes at her new address, then taken her to Battersea, where he had bigamously married her in the parish church. The couple then took up residence in Richmond.

Unfortunately, being married to Dr Smethurst did not improve Miss Bankes' digestive system in any way. For a few weeks she remained in reasonable health, though still subject to biliousness, but eventually these bouts increased in severity and she was largely confined to her bed. Smethurst appeared to be extremely concerned about his 'wife's' condition, and asked his landlady for the names of local doctors. She recommended a Dr Julius, one of Richmond's busiest practitioners, and Smethurst got in touch with him. On 3rd April 1859 Dr Julius called on Miss Bankes (or 'Mrs Smethurst', as he knew her) and gave her a thorough examination in the presence of her husband.

The visits continued over the next fortnight, but Miss Bankes did not respond to treatment. Indeed, she became progressively worse despite the enormous range of medicaments administered to her by Dr Julius. In addition she began to suffer from violent diarrhoea and complained of a burning sensation in her mouth and throat. Even the act of swallowing made her vomit. Dr Julius was an experienced practitioner, yet he had never met a case which proved so intractable. After much deliberation he came to the conclusion that Miss Bankes was being administered some irritant metallic poison, possibly arsenic or antimony. At that stage he determined to consult his partner, Dr Bird, but said nothing to him of his suspicions.

But Dr Bird, who had served in the recently-ended Crimean War and had a great deal of experience of dysentery and allied ailments, could also find no reason for the continuing symptoms. The two physicians decided to confer with Dr Smethurst and suggested calling in Dr Robert Todd, a well-known specialist in digestive ailments. Smethurst readily agreed to this course, and a few days later Dr Todd arrived and made his examination. He, too, could find no reason for Miss Bankes' continuing illness, though privately, and without mentioning it to Julius or Bird, his opinion was that she was being slowly poisoned. Smethurst's willingness to call in Dr Todd was to be given great prominence at his trial as an important aspect of his defence, and looking at the situation at a distance it certainly seems an odd thing for a guilty man to do.

During Miss Bankes' illness she had been visited on two occasions by her sister, Louisa, who had been informed of her sister's condition by Smethurst. Louisa had previously met the doctor at Rifle Terrace, and knew perfectly well that he was married. Whatever she thought of the new arrangement she kept her opinion to herself. When she came to Richmond she could not help noticing that Smethurst remained in the room the whole time she and her sister were talking, and she was told by the landlady that Smethurst insisted on taking up all the food for his wife himself and appeared to be reluctant to let the landlady into the room.

One of the subjects the sisters *did* discuss in Smethurst's presence was the recent death of an uncle, who had left them a life interest in the sum of £5,000. Miss Bankes also had her own private capital of £1,800, let out on a short-term mortgage at the time, and Smethurst discussed with the sisters the best way of increasing the interest accruing to them from these sums. After the second visit Smethurst wrote to Louisa saying that the occasion had excited her sister too much, and suggested that she did not call again for a while. He would, he said, keep her informed.

Miss Louisa was not the only one the doctor was keeping informed. It was now early April, and he wrote to his wife,

37

still at Rifle Terrace, in the most endearing terms regretting his prolonged absence 'on business' and assuring her that he would soon be home again. That the elderly Mrs Smethurst accepted this without comment and apparently did not query her husband's absence was later to give rise to the theory either that she was a party to the affair or was becoming senile.

On Sunday, 1st May, Miss Bankes' condition deteriorated to such an extent that Smethurst called urgently for the services of Drs Julius and Bird. He told them his wife was dying, but when they arrived at the house Miss Bankes had revived somewhat and was conscious. Dr Smethurst, to the surprise of the other two doctors, asked them if they knew of a solicitor in Richmond who could come that day to witness a will Miss Bankes had just made. They told him of a Mr Senior, a Richmond solicitor who lived above his offices, and Smethurst sallied forth to call on him. This was the opportunity both doctors had been waiting for, for by then they were convinced that their patient was being poisoned. Working swiftly they took samples of Miss Bankes' stool and vomit, put them into two glass jars, and sent them by their own messenger to Dr Swaine Taylor, the Home Office pathologist. With them they sent a note telling of their suspicions and requesting Dr Taylor to test the material with all possible speed for the presence of antimony or arsenic.

In the meantime Dr Smethurst had found Mr Senior at home and, with some difficulty as it was Sunday, persuaded the solicitor to accompany him to his house. The will had already been drawn up by the doctor and in it Miss Bankes left her entire capital of £1,800 to her 'dear friend, Thomas Smethurst'.

Mr Senior, on arriving at the house and seeing the condition of Miss Bankes, was understandably worried. But though she appeared to be extremely weak she was conscious and quite coherent and apparently well aware of the reason for the solicitor's presence. Senior read the will over to her slowly and carefully and was satisfied that she understood its contents. She then signed the will as 'Isabella Bankes', after addressing Smethurst in the most affectionate terms and thanking the solicitor for his trouble. With the will properly witnessed and signed Mr Senior returned home, no doubt reflecting on the peculiar circumstances of the case. Perhaps the oddest aspect of the affair was that the will was signed 'Isabella Bankes', indicating that she was perfectly aware that her 'marriage' to the doctor was not legitimate. Why a respectable Victorian spinster should have condoned such an action was never made clear, for Miss Bankes did not live long enough to explain it.

On the following day, Monday, Dr Julius received a report from Dr Taylor on the material he had sent, confirming the presence of arsenic and traces of antimony. The police were immediately informed, and by noon Smethurst had been arrested, brought before a magistrate, and charged with 'administering a toxic substance with intent to poison'. Incredible as it may seem, the doctor persuaded the magistrate that his 'wife' would suffer hardship and distress if he were not there to look after her, and was accordingly released on bail! He returned home to administer to her, but the next morning the long-suffering Isabella died. Smethurst was promptly re-arrested, this time to be charged with murder.

The trial opened at the Old Bailey on 15th August 1859 and lasted five days. The judge was Baron Pollock, who, though not on the rota for this case, had specially asked to preside. This was to have repercussions later.

There were surprises from the start, not the least being the revelation that at the time of her death Miss Bankes was seven weeks pregnant. There was also the sharp divergence of opinion shown by the seventeen medical witnesses who gave evidence, and the extraordinary mistake made by the prosecution's chief witness, Dr Swaine Taylor.

In his first and somewhat hurried examination of the contents of the two specimen bottles, Dr Taylor had found arsenic in one but not in the other. It was because of this that Smethurst had been arrested initially and later charged with murder. But when Dr Taylor carried out a full post-mortem on the body a few days later, (which resulted in twenty-eight jars containing various organs of the deceased) he could find no arsenic at all. Furthermore, when he re-examined the original two bottles he failed to confirm the presence of arsenic, though he found a minute quantity of antimony.

Dr Taylor had used Reinsch's test in his examination: this was a popular test for arsenic in Victorian times involving the use of a copper gauze which, under heat, deposited a black substance if arsenic were present. It transpired that the gauze he had used in his original test on the Sunday had already been impregnated with arsenic from a previous test, and the positive Reinsch's test on the specimens from Miss Bankes were therefore inconclusive. Immediately on discovering this he had informed the police.

It might be thought that at this point the prosecution would have been hesitant to continue with the case and would not have brought Smethurst to trial. But Swaine Taylor was an acknowledged expert in his field, and though admitting his mistake in the Reinsch's test, remained firmly convinced that Miss Bankes had died of some metallic poison, though he was careful not to specify exactly which one. His opinion was based on the condition of her internal organs, which he said could not be accounted for in any other way. The fact that no arsenic was present was due, in his view, to the patient having been given copious draughts of a solution of potassium chlorate. This, in the opinion of the pathologist, would destroy any traces of arsenic left in the body. Significantly, a large bottle of potassium chlorate solution had been found in the bedroom.

At the beginning of the trial the defence seemed to be in a very strong position. It was led by the redoubtable Serjeant Parry who began by casting doubts on the medical expertise of Dr Julius. Neither Julius nor his partner, Dr Bird, had been aware of Miss Bankes' pregnancy, and Julius testified to prescribing a remarkable variety of drugs for the sick woman which included chalk, catechu, paregoric, ipecacuanha, dilute acid, mercury, opium, quinine sulphate and dilute prussic acid. There seemed little left in the pharmacopoeia that he could have tried, but he insisted that, even had he known the patient was pregnant, his treatment would have been no different. As a result his cross-examination by Serjeant Parry was a savage one and called into question his medical skill.

PARRY: 'Are you a doctor of medicine?'
JULIUS: 'Yes.'
PARRY: 'Is yours a London degree?'
JULIUS: 'Yes.'
PARRY: 'Exactly what degree is it?'
JULIUS: 'It is the Archbishop of Canterbury's degree.'
PARRY: 'What? Can he make a doctor of medicine?'

Here the judge intervened to point out that this was, in fact, a valid degree in medicine, having been instituted by Henry VIII in 1533 under an act giving power to the Archbishop of Canterbury to confer degrees in medicine and in the arts. In any case Julius was a Licentiate of the Society of Apothecaries (a medical qualification then as now) and also a member of the College of Surgeons, so Serjeant Parry's efforts to discredit him had misfired.

The prosecution claim that Smethurst had murdered Miss Bankes in order to obtain the £1,800 left him in her will was treated with derision by the defence. In the first place he was comfortably off himself, owning property and capital to the value of £4,000 which gave him an income of £300 a year.

Secondly, in view of the life-interest in £5,000 held by Miss Bankes under her uncle's will, he could expect to benefit from this too only as long as she continued to live. He therefore had more motive to keep her alive than to see her dead. Finally there was the all-important fact that if Smethurst had really been engaged in murdering Isabella, he would scarcely have been so anxious to call in the local general practitioner, nor would he have agreed to the attendance of the specialist, Dr Todd.

Despite the fact that the prosecution had called no less than ten doctors to testify that the symptoms of the deceased and the conditon of her internal organs indicated poisoning by a metallic irritant, Parry in his turn produced seven medical experts who disagreed with this. Their contention was that all Miss Bankes' symptoms could have been the result of her pregnancy, aggravated by the extraordinary range of drugs prescribed for her by Dr Julius. Biliousness and early-morning vomiting are common conditions in early pregnancy, and in any case she had suffered in this way for some years so there was no sinister significance in it. As for the evidence of the 'expert' witness, Dr Swaine Taylor, Parry reminded the court that if the original gauze had not already been contaminated, there would have been no positive reaction for arsenic and Smethurst would probably not have been arrested at all.

Parry tried as hard as he could, but the scales were already weighted against Smethurst. Was he not revealed as a bigamist, a man who had deserted his ageing wife after thirty years of marriage and seduced an innocent spinster? Almost equally shocking to Victorian standards, had he not forced two professional men to profane the Sabbath, the solicitor, Senior, by coming to witness the will and Dr Swaine Taylor by having to perform his original test on the bottles on the holy day?

Baron Pollock's summing-up to the jury lasted nine

hours. In it he said that because Dr Swaine Taylor had made one mistake, there was no reason to discount his opinion on all other matters. He said they would have to decide if Miss Bankes had died of poisoning, and if so who was in the best position to administer it? If she was with Smethurst virtually all the time it pointed to only one conclusion. On the other hand, the judge did underline to the jury the telling evidence that no poison was found in the body. He also reminded them that although seven doctors had testified that death *might* have been due to natural causes, none of them was willing to swear that this was definitely so. However, all ten of the medical witnesses produced by the prosecution were willing to swear that death *was* due to poisoning.

In dealing with the 'improbability' of Smethurst murdering Miss Bankes, given comparatively little evidence, there was another 'improbability' that had been proved a fact.

'I do not think it more improbable than that a woman of forty-three, with an independent income, would consent to go with him and pass through a ceremony of marriage, when her own sister knew that there was a Mrs Smethurst living with him at the boarding-house. It is more improbable than anyone can understand. What you are certainly asked to believe is that, with the knowledge that he was a married man, this lady went to that church, and went through the marriage ceremony that was at once intended to make her a felon and strumpet, that she was to commit with him the crime of bigamy, in order that she might be placed in a situation remote from her friends, the scorn of one sex and the horror of another.'

As for motive, said the judge, the money was certainly sufficient, but there was also the question of the pregnancy. What were the couple to do with the baby? It might be that these two facts combined were sufficient motive for the accused to desire the death of Miss Bankes, but it was up to the jury to use their common sense in arriving at a verdict.

The jury used their common sense for exactly forty minutes, and returned with a verdict of guilty against the accused.

Smethurst was then allowed to address the court, which he did at length, going over most of the evidence again, making much of the fact that no arsenic was found in the body and the fact that, because of his own financial situation, he had no motive for murder. In his opinion death was due to natural causes, precipitated by the vast array of medicines given by Dr Julius to a woman whose constitution was already frail and who was pregnant at a comparatively advanced age. He considered the verdict totally wrong and unfair, and in his opinion the real murderer was Dr Julius.

Having allowed Smethurst his say the judge pronounced the death sentence, but curiously enough he omitted the phrase in which the accused is informed that he has no hope of mercy. This was seen by many at the time as an indication that Baron Pollock himself was not entirely happy with the outcome of the case.

The result of the Smethurst trial produced an uproar in the press and particularly so in the world of medicine. Most people (and this says a good deal for Victorian standards of justice) were reasonably sure that Smethurst *had* murdered Isabella Bankes, but very few were convinced that the case against him had been proved beyond reasonable doubt.

Said the *Medical Times & Gazette:*

> Is the prisoner guilty? We believe he is.
> Was he proved guilty? Most certainly not.

The *British Medical Journal* expressed itself in similar terms, pointing out that the division of medical opinion should have been enough to create a 'reasonable doubt' in the minds of the jury, and that that doubt should have been exercised in his favour.

The Home Secretary, Sir George Lewis, was bombarded

with letters from lawyers and doctors calling attention to the injustice of the verdict, many of the doctors professing to have intimate experience of treating dysentery and pregnancy and saying that Miss Bankes' symptoms were entirely consistent with either or both of these. Several letters drew attention to the fact that the final phase of Miss Bankes' illness, and its most acute symptoms, coincided exactly with the onset of her pregnancy.

But the most venemous abuse of all was directed at the luckless Dr Swaine Taylor for his mistake in finding arsenic when none was present. The *Dublin Medical Press* suggested that he withdraw into private life and cease to pass himself off as an 'expert witness' in any court of law.

For weeks the controversy raged, finally culminating in a petition to the Home Secretary for a free pardon, drawn up by Smethurst's solicitor. Amongst the many points covered was a criticism of the hostile summing-up of the judge to the jury, that Baron Pollock had particularly requested to take the case, and that he and Dr Swaine Taylor were close friends.

Surprisingly, at this state the original Mrs Smethurst made an appearance on the scene and came to the aid of her husband with her own petition as follows:

To the Queen's Most Excellent Majesty.
The Humble Petition of Mary Smethurst, the wife of Thomas Smethurst, Doctor of Medicine, a prisoner now lying under sentence of death in the County Gaol of Surrey.

1. That your petitioner is now in the seventy-fourth year of her age, that she was on the 10th day of March, 1828, married at St Mark's Church, Kennington, to the prisoner, who was then twenty-four years old and your petitioner in her forty-fourth year and a spinster.

2. That for thirty years your petitioner lived happily

with her husband from whom she always received the tenderest kindness and affection.

3. That in or about the month of April 1858, your petitioner and her husband went to reside in the boarding-house of Mrs Mary Smith at 4 Rifle Terrace, Bayswater, and so continued to do until the end of November 1858.

4. That in September in that year the deceased lady, Isabella Bankes, came to live in the same house, and that in November 1858, your petitioner observed much familiarity between her husband and that lady; that in consequence of an intimation from the landlady, Mrs Smith, to Miss Bankes, on that subject, the latter quitted her house on 29th November and that the prisoner quitted at about the same time.

5. That your petitioner was grieved beyond all endurance at the departure of her husband with that lady, who well knew that the petitioner was his wife when she went away with the prisoner, as they had all been in daily association in the said boarding-house for about ten weeks.

6. That your petitioner, during thirty years that she lived with her husband, was during several illnesses attended by him with the most constant care, performing the duties of doctor and of nurse.

7. That he has always been of a most humane and animated disposition, charitable, benevolent, and generous to his connections. That in all the years of their connection your petitioner never knew her husband to do any act of cruelty or unkindness to any living creature, excepting in the quitting of your petitioner as related.

8. That the prisoner is a person of economical and temperate habits, possessed a sufficient income from house property at Bayswater and at Brompton for all

his wants, and saving usually a surplus from his income, so that he was in no pecuniary difficulty or temptation to commit a foul murder in the chance of obtaining a few hundred pounds.

9. That the first advances came from Miss Bankes to the prisoner, who unhappily yielded to the temptation; but that for thirty years his moral conduct has been irreproachable.

10. That your petitioner is perfectly confident of the entire innocence of her husband of the crime of murder and that she is equally certain that he has been convicted and placed in his present awful peril by a combination of circumstances not justly leading to the conclusion of his guilt.

11. That if he should be executed your petitioner is convinced a most horrible judicial murder will be committed.

Your petitioner therefore humbly prays your Most Gracious Majesty will be pleased to exercise in this extraordinary case your Royal prerogative of mercy, and, in granting her husband a full and free pardon, remove the stain which is cast upon him by this unjust conviction and save his life.

And your petitioner will ever pray etc.

MARY SMETHURST

There is little doubt that these petitions, coupled with the continuing public outcry, put the Home Secretary in a difficult position. There was no Court of Criminal Appeal in existence at the time, and he evidently felt himself unfitted to assess accurately the value of the medical evidence. He therefore decided to turn the whole affair over to Sir Benjamin Brodie, one of Queen Victoria's surgeons and one of the most eminent medical men of his day.

This was an odd thing to do, for the case rested on much

more than the medical evidence, and the Home Secretary was asking a doctor, albeit an eminent one, to act both as judge and jury and review the entire sequence of events.

Sir Benjamin took his duties seriously and re-examined all the evidence from beginning to end. His final decision was that the prosecution had failed to make out a convincing case against Smethurst and he recommended that he be granted a free pardon. The Home Secretary agreed and the pardon was granted, much to the delight of the medical profession. But the Home Secretary had a last gibe at the doctors when he gave the reasons for his action, stressing that Smethurst's wrongful conviction had not been the result of any fault in the legal machinery, but was due to the inability of several experienced physicians to agree on a diagnosis.

Smethurst was a free man once more, but not for long. He rejoined his long-suffering and surprisingly charitable wife in Pimlico, but in November 1859 was arrested again, this time for his bigamous marriage to Isabella Bankes. For the second time in a few weeks Smethurst saw the inside of the Old Bailey. He was found guilty and sentenced to twelve months' hard labour, which he did in the new 'model' prison at Holloway.

With all the publicity that had surrounded the Smethurst affair, one might have expected the doctor to maintain a comparatively low profile on his release. But his first action was to attempt to obtain damages from the police for what he called his 'wrongful imprisonment and deprivation of liberty'. Not surprisingly, he failed.

He then proceeded to put Miss Bankes' will to probate, but this action was strenuously opposed by relatives who took an extremely poor view of the fact that the man they were convinced had murdered Isabella should profit by his action.

The result was a two-day hearing in the Court of Probate, at the end of which the jury found that Miss Bankes' will was properly signed and witnessed, and that as the doctor had not been convicted of murder there was no legal reason why he should not inherit the £1,800.

Smethurst returned to his legal wife, collected the money, and vanished from the scene.

Was he really a murderer? We shall never know. Apart from the medical evidence (which was shaky, to say the least) there was little else to point to his guilt. Smethurst had money of his own and was comfortably off without Miss Bankes' money. In addition the interest on her £5,000 investment would cease if she died. Calling in Dr Julius, and later agreeing to have Miss Bankes examined by the specialist Dr Todd, does not seem to be the action of a guilty man. Finally there was the important fact that no arsenic was found anywhere in the body and that Smethurst never had arsenic in his possession.

If he *did* poison Miss Bankes, and succeeded in eliminating all traces of arsenic by giving her copious draughts of potassium chlorate solution, why did he do it? The most likely reason may well have been the one hinted at by the judge in his summing-up — that Miss Bankes was pregnant, and murdering her was the only way he could rid himself of this awkward complication.

That Smethurst was something of a rogue is well-established. But that he went as far as committing murder was shown to be a question of doubt in 1859, and we are no nearer the truth of the matter over a hundred years later.

3

Edward Pritchard

(1825-1865)

The extraordinary hypocrisy which is for many such a feature of the Victorian age is well exemplified in the story of Dr Edward Pritchard of Glasgow. Amongst the rich haul of Victorian murderers, few can surpass the humbug and hypocrisy of Pritchard, a man who combined homicide with an exaggerated piety, fornication with Freemasonry, and who was possessed of an imagination so wonderfully powerful that even those who knew him for only a short time quickly turned from him in disgust.

Typical of the times, his wife seems to have condoned his various amours in return for a comfortable home and an adequate allowance, though his sexual proclivities were well known to their friends. Even his mother-in-law, though well aware that Pritchard was frequently unfaithful to her daughter, kept her mouth shut when she discovered the obvious liaison existing between the doctor and a sixteen-year-old maid. However well-intended this silence may have been, it did not save her from an exceedingly painful death.

Dr Edward Pritchard was born in Southsea, Hampshire, in 1825. He qualified as a doctor in 1848 and, following the family naval tradition, went to sea as a ship's surgeon for two years, visiting the Mediterranean and the Middle East. Back in Portsmouth in 1850 he met and married Mary Jane Taylor, who was on holiday in the town from Edinburgh. The honeymoon was brief as he had to go to sea again for another year.

The Taylor family was wealthy (Mary Jane's father was a

retired silk-merchant in Edinburgh) and both her parents seem to have taken immediately to their son-in-law. They were naturally concerned that his duties would force him to be away from his wife for long periods, and they determined to do something about it.

Certainly Pritchard was a charmer — tall, good-looking, and, though prematurely bald, sporting an enormous beard and side-whiskers. Women were instantly attracted to him, and he was attracted to women — a dangerous attribute for a man soon to take up his duties as a general practitioner, and one which would eventually cause his downfall.

To avoid him having to go to sea, the wealthy Taylors decided to provide him with a practice, and a suitable one was eventually found at Humnanby in Yorkshire. Pritchard set up his plate, and for a year or two managed to maintain a reasonably successful practice in the town. Gradually, however, rumours began to circulate about his somewhat un-ethical attitude towards the more attractive female patients, and the practice began to dwindle. His wife seemed either unaware or unconcerned with the situation. When an irate husband threatened to begin divorce proceedings as a result of Pritchard's association with his wife, the doctor decided to sell the practice and leave Humnanby.

His fellow physicians were not sorry to see him go, for his reputation with women, his lies and his constant boasting had made him notorious and cast a slur on the whole medical profession. As a member of the Yorkshire Freemasons he took to wearing his Masonic robes in public, and using his membership for advertising purposes, something totally forbidden by that ancient and honourable organization. Said the *Sheffield Telegraph* later:

They found his imagination over-ran the limits of probability as much as his expenditure over-ran his means. He left with no credit, only creditors. He was fluent, plausible, amorous, politely impudent and singularly untruthful. The prettiest liar ever met with.

In 1858 he left Humnanby and, quitting his wife and five children, attempted to re-organize his finances by going to sea again for a year. When he returned he decided to acquire a practice in Glasgow, and he and his family moved in to 11 Berkeley Terrace in 1860.

Unfortunately, news of his escapades in Yorkshire had preceded him. Members of his own profession ostracized him and refused to admit him into their circle. Even so his conceit and vanity were such that he decided to apply for the then vacant Andersonian Chair of Surgery at Edinburgh University. As nobody would sponsor him for this important post he calmly set about writing his own testimonials, forging the signatures of various eminent surgeons, none of whom he had ever met. Needless to say, he did not get the appointment.

Thick-skinned as ever, and with a practice that could scarcely support him, he embarked on a series of lecture tours in the Glasgow and Edinburgh areas purporting to describe his adventures in foreign parts. The more gullible members of the public flocked to hear him, particularly when he began his talks with phrases such as, 'I have plucked the eagles from their eyries in the deserts of Arabia, and hunted the Nubian lion in the prairies of North America.'

It is doubtful if he would have recognized a Nubian lion had he met one in the street, but his audiences loved it and for some time he was a great success. He also claimed close friendship with the then hero of the day, Guiseppe Garibaldi, and proudly exhibited a walking-stick engraved with the words, 'To my good friend Dr Pritchard from his friend General Garibaldi.' It so happened that most of his acquaintances remembered seeing him with the cane long before he had had it engraved. This sort of thing did not impress the residents of Glasgow who were already aware of his lies and boasting. Nor were they impressed by his habit of offering patients and casual acquaintances photographic cartes-de-visite of himself, occasionally asking for a small donation to defray expenses.

His first brush with the law came on 5th May 1863, when a mysterious fire broke out in a bedroom at the house in Berkeley Terrace. Mary Jane Pritchard and the children were away in Edinburgh at the time and the doctor and a young maid were the only people on the premises. At three in the morning a fire was spotted in the maid's bedroom and the fire brigade called.

Pritchard was already up and dressed, claiming that he had just come home. The fire was quickly put out, but not before the girl's body was found in the smouldering bedroom; at first glance she seemed to have died peacefully in her sleep, undisturbed by the conflagration.

Pritchard described the affair as 'a melancholy accident' but the general opinion at the time, also shared by the police, was that the girl had died because she had previously been drugged, though there was never any proof of this.

Nor was there ever any proof of the valuable items of jewellery Pritchard maintained had been lost in the fire, and for which he claimed from the insurance company. The company refused to pay and Pritchard withdrew his claim, but not before there was talk of taking proceedings against him for fraud. In the event no action was taken, but by that time the doctor had outstayed his welcome in that part of Glasgow, and once again decided to move on. In May 1864 he set about establishing a practice in Royal Crescent, then part of Sauchiehall Street. This house, No. 22, was to be the scene of the dramatic events destined to bring Pritchard face to face with the hangman just over a year later.

The household at Royal Crescent consisted of the doctor, his wife and four of their five children (the oldest, Fanny, seems to have been permanently resident with her grandparents in Edinburgh). There was the cook, Catherine Lattimer, who had been with the family for ten years and a young maid, Mary M'Leod, who had replaced the victim of the 'melancholy accident'. To augment his income the doctor also had two medical students, James Connell and Daniel King, as lodgers.

There was plenty to do in the house and Mrs Pritchard did it well. Now thirty-seven years old, Mary Jane was a strong and healthy woman, devoted to her family and her husband, and willing to ignore his constant lies and boastfulness and even to overlook the very obvious affair between him and the sixteen-year-old Mary M'Leod.

In October 1864 Mrs Pritchard suddenly became ill. She began to suffer from stomach cramps and biliousness, and for a large part of the time was confined to her room. She was able to write to her mother, Mrs Taylor, in Edinburgh and that lady wrote back immediately urging her daughter to come to Edinburgh for a time until she felt better.

At first the doctor was unwilling to let her go, writing to Mrs Taylor, 'I do not think we could manage without her unless Dear Grandma could come and take charge while she is away.' But eventually he gave way, and his wife travelled to Edinburgh on 26th November. During the visit her health improved so rapidly that she was able to return home on 22nd December and supervise the preparations for the Christmas festivities which were to include a 'juvenile party'.

Christmas went off as planned, but in the first week of January 1865 all Mary Jane's symptoms returned. Everything she ate or drank was rejected, she lost weight and steadily became weaker and weaker. She could not understand what was happening, and frequently commented on how well she had felt in Edinburgh and how wretched at home in Glasgow.

Pritchard could not have been more attentive to his wife,

supervising the preparation of the small amounts of food she was able to take and expressing grave concern at the continuance of her mysterious illness.

At length, on 5th February, Pritchard wrote to his wife's cousin, a retired physician called Cowan who lived in Edinburgh, asking him to come and give an opinion on his wife's condition. Dr Cowan duly arrived, but his only suggestion was that Mrs Pritchard should have mustard poultices applied to her abdomen, and be given small quantities of champagne as a 'tonic'. At the same time he was worried enough to contact Mrs Taylor as soon as he returned to Edinburgh and urge her to go to Glasgow to look after her daughter.

Before Mrs Taylor could arrive, Mary Jane had a particularly violent attack one night, with bouts of cramp which made her scream with pain. So great was her distress that at midnight Pritchard sent a message to a Dr Gairdner who, though not a general practitioner but a University professor, lived just round the corner and was the nearest physician available.

On his arrival Dr Gairdner questioned Pritchard about his wife's illness and was told that she had been ill for several weeks, and was probably suffering from catalepsy, a disease producing a death-like trance. This diagnosis by Pritchard was so bizarre that it caused Gairdner to have serious doubts about the other's competence as a physician. He was also horrified to hear that Mrs Pritchard had been prescribed champagne, which he described as 'very bad treatment' and put her on an extremely light diet with no alcoholic stimulants whatsoever.

Like Dr Gowan, Dr Gairdner had never been to the house before and was worried that Mary Jane was not receiving the correct treatment at the hands of her husband. He accordingly wrote to the sick woman's brother, with whom he had qualified, at Penrith, suggesting that she spend some

55

time with him. But on this occasion Pritchard was adamant. In the first place, he argued, she was far too weak to travel, and in any case 'Dear Grandma' would be arriving at any moment to look after her.

Mrs Taylor, a robust and somewhat overbearing lady of seventy, duly arrived at Royal Crescent and immediately took over the running of the house. She was also a singularly perceptive old woman, and it did not take her long to recognize the relationship existing between her son-in-law and Mary M'Leod. But, for some reason, like her daughter she kept silent.

Mrs Taylor's many alterations in the running of the household included banning Pritchard from sleeping with his wife, and he was relegated to an upstairs room. This, presumably, he did not mind too much as it made access to Mary easier during the night. Mrs Taylor also decided that her daughter should be fed on tapioca. A pound of this was duly purchased, in an unsealed bag, and left on the hall table for some hours before being taken into the kitchen. When a cupful was prepared by Mary it was first tasted by Mrs Taylor. She was immediately and violently sick. She said she must have acquired the same illness as her daughter, and the remainder of the tapioca was not used but returned to the pantry. Its next public appearance was to be in court.

A few evenings later Mrs Taylor, having had supper with the family, spent the evening in the consulting-room writing letters, almost certainly to various medical friends, on the subject of her daughter. At half-past nine she went as usual to her daughter's room, prepared to spend the night with her. Half an hour later the violent ringing of the bedroom bell alerted the staff, and Mary and the cook rushed upstairs to see what was amiss.

They fully expected to find that Mrs Pritchard had taken a turn for the worse, but to their astonishment it was Mrs Taylor who needed assistance, lying apparently unconscious in her chair by the bed, her head lolling on her chest. Mary Jane was in a distressed, semi-hysterical condition and the women immediately sent for Dr Pritchard. He calmly asked Mary to fetch Dr Paterson, a well-known gynaecologist, who, like Dr Gairdner, happened to live close by. It is not known why he did not send for Dr Gairdner again, but it may well be that he found this physician's hostility and criticism not to his liking.

Pritchard and the cook then got Mrs Taylor on to the bed with her daughter, after which Pritchard went downstairs to receive Dr Paterson. When the gynaecologist arrived Pritchard, true to form, gave him a totally inaccurate account of what had happened. According to him, Mrs Taylor had been writing letters in the consulting-room, had been taken ill and fallen off her chair, and had then been carried upstairs to the bedroom. He also told Paterson that he attributed his mother-in-law's illness to gastric fever and hinted that she was rather fond of the bottle.

When Dr Paterson saw Mrs Taylor he was convinced that she had not very long to live. She regained consciousness for a moment and Pritchard slapped her on the back and cried, 'You are getting better, my darling!' to which Paterson replied 'Never in this world.'

Pritchard then told Paterson that Mrs Taylor was in the habit of taking large doses of Battley's Sedative Solution, a popular Victorian patent medicine consisting mainly of opium in a solution of alcohol. Indeed, a half-empty bottle of Battley's was found in Mrs Taylor's pocket, and Pritchard expressed horror and surprise at the amount that had been taken.

Paterson by this time was also alarmed at the state in which he found Mary Jane Pritchard, and, good diagnostician that he was, formed the immediate impression that she was suffering from poisoning by antimony. He said nothing, and being unable to do anything more for Mrs

Taylor, returned home. Just before one in the morning he received an urgent summons to come to the Pritchard house again, but refused to go as he felt he could be of no further assistance. For this and his later lack of action he was to be severely reprimanded.

Mrs Taylor died soon after one o'clock and Pritchard recorded the event there and then in his diary:

'February 25. Saturday. – About 1 a.m. in this morning, passing away calmly – peacefully – and the features retaining a life-like character – so finely drawn was the transition that it would be impossible to determine with decision the moment when life may said to be departed.'

It was just a fortnight since Mrs Taylor had arrived at Royal Crescent, hale and hearty and determined to nurse her daughter back to health. Little did she know that Pritchard had decided otherwise. Mary Jane was extremely upset at the death of her mother, and her condition deteriorated considerably.

Later on that Saturday Mr Taylor, 'Dear Grandma's' bereaved husband, arrived in Glasgow in response to a telegram he had received from Pritchard advising him of his wife's death. Still dazed and uncomprehending, he was sent by Pritchard to Dr Paterson to obtain a death certificate, Paterson being the last physician to have seen the dead woman. But Dr Paterson, for reasons which he did not divulge at the time, refused to provide the document, so Pritchard himself wrote out the death certificate, giving the cause as 'Paralysis 12 hrs. Apoplexy 1 hr.' 'Paralysis' was certainly a very odd way of accounting for the death of a robust woman who, only an hour before, had been capable of walking upstairs unaided. It was also nonsense medically, for as any practitioner should have known, paralysis invariably *follows* apoplexy and does not precede it.

On 2nd March Pritchard and Mr Taylor accompanied the body to Edinburgh for the funeral, and Pritchard dutifully wrote in his diary:

'2nd March: Buried Mrs Taylor, poor Dear Grandma, in Grange Cemetery, fifty yards from the entrance, to the left – near the Lovers' Lane.'

Pritchard had asked Dr Paterson to look in on his wife while he was away. When Paterson did call, he found the patient in an even more pitiable condition than before. He was now even more certain that she was suffering from the effects of antimony poisoning. But, though he was alone with her, he made no mention of this fact and gave her no warning, nor did he take a sample of her urine, which would have been the normal thing to do under the circumstances.

What Paterson did do, however, was consult various medical colleagues and solicit their opinion. On 4th March, he received a blank form from the District Registrar with a request to supply details of Mrs Taylor's death and wrote back:

Windsor Place, 4th March, 1865

Dear Sir,

I am surprised that I am called upon to certify *the cause of death* in this case. I only saw the person for a few minutes a very short period before her death. She seemed to be under some narcotic, but Dr Pritchard, who was present from the first moment of her illness until death occurred, and which happened in his own house, may certify the cause. The death was certainly sudden, unexpected and to me mysterious.

I am, dear Sir,
Yours faithfully,
James Paterson, MD.

Despite this obvious hint that all was not well, the District Registrar took no action and even destroyed the letter. Fortunately the methodical Dr Paterson had kept a copy.

Since the death of his mother-in-law, Pritchard had once again taken his rightful place in his wife's bed, with Mary M'Leod sleeping on a couch at the foot of the bed. The doctor reverted to supervising the preparation of all Mary Jane's food, and on 13th March gave the maid some soft cheese with which to tempt her mistress. After Mrs Pritchard had tasted it she said there was something wrong and asked Mary to taste it. This she did, and found it 'hot, like pepper'. She said it burned her throat and induced a raging thirst. The cheese was returned to the kitchen, and later the cook ate a portion. The result of this was a violent stomach reaction which prostrated her for some hours.

A few days later the doctor prepared a jug of camomile tea for his wife; instead of having a soothing effect, it induced even more vomiting. Later that night he suggested to the cook that his wife might benefit from drinking an egg-flip. He watched the woman prepare this and then went into his consulting-room for the purpose, he said, of getting some whisky to put into it. After he had added the whisky, and while his back was turned, the cook sampled the mixture and found it exceedingly bitter. The doctor thereupon added two lumps of sugar and took it up to his wife. Once again the result was immediate and prolonged vomiting and stomach cramps. Mary Jane Pritchard's agony was not to last much longer.

On Friday, 17th March, soon after noon, she rang the bell in her bedroom three times. It was Mary's duty to answer it, but as she was apparently not available the cook went to the consulting-room to fetch the doctor. She found the door slightly ajar, and when she pushed against it it was obvious that somebody on the other side was holding it in position. She turned to go upstairs, but on looking back was just in time to see the doctor emerge from the room closely followed by a distinctly dishevelled Mary. The doctor then went upstairs to see his wife and gave her something from a glass which seemed to relieve her distress.

Later that day, at about five o'clock, Mary Jane was found out of bed crawling about on the upstairs landing. She was delirious and kept pointing down the stairs saying 'There is my poor dear mother, dead again.' With some difficulty Pritchard, Mary and the cook managed to get her back to bed, and at 7.45 p.m. Pritchard sent an urgent message to Dr Paterson.

When Paterson arrived he was greatly alarmed. Mrs Pritchard's eyes were sunken and bloodshot, her cheeks hollow and her body emaciated. She continued to rave and talk nonsense. Paterson prescribed a simple sleeping-draught to be given immediately, but Pritchard said this was not possible as he had no medicines or drugs on the premises except for a small amount of chloroform and the unconsumed portion of Mrs Taylor's bottle of Battley's Sedative. Paterson accordingly returned home. It was the last time he was to see Mrs Pritchard alive.

Soon after one o'clock in the morning Mrs Pritchard went into a violent paroxsym and died in her husband's arms. He seemed stunned and ordered Mary to fetch some hot poultices. The cook, who was also present, said it was too late for that. 'Is she dead, then?' asked the distraught husband, to which the cook replied 'You should know better than me!' Pritchard became overwrought, clasping the dead woman to his chest and crying 'Come back, come back, my darling Mary Jane. Do not leave your dear Edward!' But Mary Jane had already left, and, finally convinced of this, the doctor hurried downstairs to make the inevitable entry in his diary.

'18, Saturday: Died here at 1 a.m. Mary Jane, my own beloved wife, aged 38 years. No torment surrounded her bedside, but like a calm peaceful Lamb of God passed Minnie away. May God and Jesus, Holy Ghost — one in three, welcome Minne. Prayer on prayer till mine be o'er, everlasting love. Save us, dear Lord, for thy dear Son.'

In certifying the death of Mary Jane, Pritchard this time took no chances. He provided the certificate himself, giving gastric fever as the cause of death. For the second time in three weeks a funeral procession wended its way from the Pritchard home in Glasgow to Edinburgh, where the body lay at the Taylors' house before being interred two days later.

This gave Pritchard the opportunity for one of his most macabre performances when, immediately before the funeral, he insisted that the coffin lid be raised so that he could implant a final kiss on the cold lips of his dead wife. At the grave-side he completely broke down 'and exhibited a great deal of feeling', being restrained only by the use of force from throwing himself on to the coffin. Whatever contribution Pritchard had made to the medical profession it is obvious he was a great loss to the stage.

On the morning of Mary Jane's funeral in Edinburgh the Procurator Fiscal in Glasgow received the following anonymous communication:

Glasgow, March 18th, 1865

Sir,

Dr Pritchard's mother-in-law died suddenly and unexpectedly about three weeks ago in his house in Sauchiehall Street, Glasgow, under circumstances at least very suspicious. His wife died today, also suddenly and unexpectedly and under circumstances equally suspicious. We think it right to draw your attention to the above, as the proper person to take action in the matter and see justice done.

Yours etc.
amor JUSTITAE

It is fairly certain that this letter was written by Dr Paterson after further consultation with colleagues, but this the doctor always denied. For a man who was so concerned about medical etiquette this is not surprising.

This time action was swift, and on Pritchard's return from Edinburgh he was met at the station by Superintendent McCall of the Glasgow City Police. He was arrested on suspicion of murder and taken to Police Headquarters. Much to the embarrassment of those present not only did he deny the charge but fell on his knees and invited the police to join him in prayer! He was somewhat put out when nobody accepted his invitation.

Police enquiries got under way and a preliminary post-mortem was conducted on the body of Mrs Pritchard. No external features were found which could account for her death, but the full post-mortem established without any doubt that she had died as a result of antimony poisoning. Virtually every organ in her body showed the presence of the poison and even her bed-clothes were tainted with it. Pritchard denied ever giving his wife antimony internally, but did admit that he had once applied a liniment containing the poison to her neck when she had a swelling there.

Pritchard was thereupon formally charged with the murder of Mary Jane, and as a result of the statement he made to the police Mary M'Leod was also arrested and charged with complicity in the crime. After two days of questioning it was decided that there was insufficient evidence to hold her, and she was released to testify against her lover in court later.

In the meantime the body of Mrs Taylor had also been exhumed, and tests indicated that she, too, had died of antimonial poisoning, though a lesser quantity was found in the body. Pritchard was then charged with the additional murder of his mother-in-law. 'I never administered poison to her,' said he. 'I did and still do believe that she died from paralysis and apoplexy.'

He maintained his innocence of both murders and constantly exclaimed 'Who could have done such a dastardly thing?' Even his gaolers were impressed by his apparent piety and belief in his own innocence, for the doctor had always been a most convincing liar and could (for a short time at least) produce a most favourable impression on both sexes. He continued to put the blame on Mary M'Leod who, he said, had done away with his wife in the hope that he would marry her as soon as he was free.

The trial began on 3rd July 1865 before the High Court of Justiciary in Edinburgh presided over by Lord Justice Clerk Inglis. From the beginning it was rather a one-sided affair, the defence having very little evidence on which to work apart from Pritchard's vehement denials and calls to the Almighty to prove his innocence. But there was too much evidence against him. The packet of tapioca left in the larder had been analysed and found to contain antimony, and the bottle of Battley's Sedative, already containing opium as one of its ingredients, was found to have had both antimony and aconite added to it.

It was difficult to believe that a man who protested great devotion to his wife and similar affection for his mother-in-law could really be guilty of such cold-blooded behaviour, and the defence grasped any straw to prove this. One such straw was the bottle of Battley's, for here the defence suggested that Mrs Taylor was so addicted to the mixture that it may well have been the opium that killed her, and that therefore whoever had added the other ingredients was not a murderer!

Despite the fact that Pritchard had told Paterson that he could not prepare his wife a sleeping draught as he had no medicines in the house, this proved to be untrue. In a cupboard in the consulting-room were packets and bottles containing atropine, antimony, laudanum, coniine (a nicotine-like alkaloid), morphine and digitalis. Furthermore, all of these had been purchased from local chemists between September 1864 and March 1865, and in quantities far greater than would normally be required by even the busiest general practitioner.

The evidence of Mary M'Leod was an important feature of the trial. It was revealed that she had been seduced by Pritchard at the age of fifteen and that later she had conceived a child that had been aborted by him. Part of her evidence, though it was confirmed by Pritchard, was difficult to believe. Mrs Pritchard had clearly known of the affair between her husband and Mary. After the abortion Mary had wanted to leave, but Mrs Pritchard had begged her to stay, saying that she knew her husband was a 'nasty, dirty man' but that she would speak to him and stop him pestering the maid. Mary also said that Pritchard had promised to marry her, and the cook gave evidence that she had heard Mary talking of the time when she would 'take Mrs Pritchard's place'.

This evidence was used to advantage by both sides at the trial, the prosecution maintaining that it gave Pritchard a reason for murdering his wife, the defence contending that it gave Mary a motive for murdering her mistress.

Looking at the facts objectively, it seemed most unlikely that the semi-literate Mary could have had sufficient medical knowledge to know what she was doing and to administer poison slowly and methodically over several weeks. Nor was it very likely that Pritchard, a professional man, would ever have married an uneducated servant-girl, and his 'promise', if it were ever made, was most probably what has been called elsewhere 'the small change of the seducer'.

Nor was there any financial motive for the killings, for Pritchard, though slightly overdrawn at the bank, had recently borrowed £500 from his in-laws and there is little doubt that that generous family would have been willing to provide more if a financial crisis had developed. The question of motive in the Pritchard case remains something of an enigma though, of course, motive does not have to be proved to convict a murderer. It is very probable that the murder of Mrs Taylor came about because Pritchard realized she was getting suspicious of her daughter's illness and because she knew about the affair with Mary. As for Mary Jane Pritchard, the doctor had probably tired of her, and in his eyes she stood between him and more exciting sexual adventures.

Dr Paterson, who had suspected from the first that Mrs Pritchard was being poisoned with antimony, did not appear in a very good light at the trial. He said that he had not voiced his suspicions to Mrs Pritchard partly for fear of frightening her, and partly because of the fear that she might repeat the allegation to her husband, landing Paterson in a legal action with possibly heavy damages for libel. In any case, he said, it was a question of medical etiquette.

The judge was particularly severe on Paterson, and said in his summing-up:

I care not for professional etiquette or professional rules. There is a rule of life and a consideration that is far higher than these — and that is, the duty every right-minded citizen owes to his neighbour to prevent the destruction of human life, and in that duty I cannot but say that Dr Paterson failed.

However, in fairness to Dr Paterson it must be remembered that he *did* draw the attention of the District Registrar to the matter immediately after his first visit, even if his letter was ignored.

At the end of the trial the jury were presented with two hypotheses. There was no doubt that Mrs Pritchard had been murdered at Royal Crescent, but by whom? The prosecution case was that the murderer was Pritchard, the defence case that it was Mary M'Leod. On this point the judge had this to say:

> We should have little doubt which was the servant and which was the master . . . and that if two were concerned you could have very little doubt who prepared it and who set it on the other. And, in fact, if you should arrive at that conclusion, every article that the prisoner's counsel alluded to for the purpose of showing the guilt of Mary M'Leod would be an article of evidence to implicate the prisoner at the bar.

At the end of the summing-up the jury retired for forty-five minutes, returning with a verdict of guilty against Pritchard on both counts. The judge sentenced the prisoner to death, and Pritchard bowed politely to both judge and jury before being taken to the cells.

No appeal was lodged, for nobody expected one would succeed. In the condemned cell Pritchard was a model, if somewhat eccentric, prisoner, spending his last days praying loudly and copying out texts from the Bible which he presented to his gaolers. As a member of the Scottish Episcopal Church he was visited by two clergymen of that faith who attempted to make him confess his crimes. Imaginative and a liar to the end, Pritchard made two 'confessions', neither of which was believed. In the first he admitted to poisoning his wife with antimony but with the connivance of Mary. In the second he said that he had killed his wife with chloroform, again with Mary's help, but strongly denied murdering Mrs Taylor. According to him he had added the antimony and aconite to the bottle of Battley's Sedative *after* her death in order to draw attention to the dangers of taking large doses of that medicine!

Only at the third attempt did he finally confess to murdering both women in the manner the prosecution had outlined in court. Even so he managed to scandalize both clerics by remarking 'I now understand how Jesus suffered from the unbelief of men in his Word.' This incredible piece of blasphemy was too much for one of the clergymen, who broke down completely and had to be assisted, sobbing, from the condemned cell. Pritchard could not understand what had upset him.

He was hanged on Glasgow Green at eight o'clock in the morning of 28th July 1865, before a crowd of several thousand spectators. He walked bravely to the scaffold, head erect 'as if marching to the sound of music' as one eye-witness reported. On the scaffold he attempted to address the crowd, but was stopped by the prison authorities, no doubt to his great disappointment. His last words were addressed to his own parish priest, who was in attendance, congratulating him on being considerate enough to wear his gown and bands for the occasion.

It was the last public hanging in Glasgow.

4

Henry George Lamson

(1849-1882)

The years between 1855 and 1882 are noteworthy for the large number of medical murders that took place during that period. What caused this sudden rise in the medical crime rate is not known, but it may well be connected with numerous experiments on the action of poisonous vegetable alkaloids. Most general practitioners knew of these experiments and all had access to these poisons. It was therefore perhaps not too surprising that those doctors with homicidal tendencies should extend the experiments to the taking of human life.

Some of the doctors involved, like Palmer and Pritchard, were careless and stupid. Others were more cunning both in their choice of poison and the method of its administration. Of the latter kind was the young Dr Lamson who carefully chose a poison, aconitine, about which very little was known at the time apart from the fact that it was highly toxic. In addition, he tried to hoodwink the police by providing what seemed an obvious clue as to how it was administered while in reality he chose a much more devious method of introducing the poison.

It is a pity that Lamson's undoubted intelligence was not wholly centred on his work as a doctor. Early in his career he was a credit to his profession but, as he himself was to admit later, a fatal addiction to morphine proved his downfall.

He was born in 1849 and from early childhood was of an adventurous disposition. When he told his parents that he wished to take up medicine as a career, they were delighted.

They were not quite so pleased at the news that their son wanted to undergo his medical training in Paris, but, through various business contacts of his father, all was arranged and in 1867 he took up residence as a medical student in Paris in the heady atmosphere of the Second Empire.

He was twenty-one in 1870, a handsome and pleasant-faced young man, liked by all who had contact with him, and extremely enthusiastic about his work. When the Franco-Prussian war erupted that year, he immediately volunteered for service in the French Ambulance Corps where he distinguished himself by his devotion to duty, as he continued to do during the terrible days of the Commune that followed.

With the war over and the civil disturbances dying down he resumed his medical studies and qualified as a doctor in Paris in 1874. He then joined the staff of the Paris Maternity Hospital, where he worked until 1876. In that year came the uprising in the Balkans against the dominance of Turkey, and the adventurous doctor gave up his hospital post and enlisted in the British Red Cross in Serbia. When Romania came into the war he joined the staff of the British Hospital in Bucharest. For his work in the field he was subsequently decorated by both the Serbian and Romanian governments.

After such an active career it was not surprising that the young doctor finally desired a little peace and quiet. He returned to England early in 1878 and while visiting relatives in London met an attractive young lady named Kate John. The attraction was mutual, and later that year the couple were married.

Kate was one of five children. Her parents had died some years previously and she was a ward in Chancery. Originally there had been two girls and three boys, but at the time of her marriage one brother, Herbert, was already dead; there remained one married sister, Margaret Chapman, and two brothers, Henry and Percy. Henry John died suddenly of an undetermined stomach complaint just a year after his sister had married Lamson. This left one surviving brother, Percy John, fifteen years old in 1878 and a cripple, suffering from curvature of the spine and paralysis of the lower limbs. He was a pupil at a special school in Wimbledon.

Old Mrs John, the children's mother, had died in 1869. The widow of a wealthy Manchester merchant, her will provided that the estate be divided equally between the five children, but should any of them die before the age of twenty-one, their share was to be divided amongst the others. Henry John was only twenty when he died in 1879 and the three remaining children, Kate (usually known as Kitty), her sister Margaret Chapman and brother Percy all inherited a fairly large sum. Young Percy's assets in 1879 were calculated to be in the region of £3,000 and, in accordance with the will, should he, too, die before reaching twenty-one this amount would be shared by his two sisters. As the Married Woman's Property Act had not then been passed the money would, in fact, go to the husbands, and each would benefit by about £1,500.

Of the two brothers-in-law, Lamson was most in need of extra money. On returning to England, and immediately after his marriage, he had attempted to establish himself as a general practitioner and had bought a practice in Rotherfield, Sussex. When events did not develop as rapidly as he would have wished he had the ingenious idea of adding to his name-plate the name of a highly popular doctor in a nearby town, to give the impression they were in partnership. The doctor concerned reported Lamson to the British Medical Association, and the resultant publicity forced Lamson to leave Sussex.

He bought another practice in South London, but this too failed to come up to expectations and Lamson soon put it on the market. When prospective purchasers were on the premises, he hired some of the local unemployed to ring his doorbell at frequent intervals and ask for medical attention.

This kind of behaviour seemed far removed from the pleasant and efficient young man who had worked so assiduously in Paris and the Balkans. The truth was that whilst in Serbia the young doctor had been experimenting with morphine, and was now well on the way to becoming an addict. Added to this was a history of mental instability in his father's family, and his curious behaviour from the time he returned to England and married was later to be used as an indication that he was becoming insane.

Early in 1880 he bought a third practice in Bournemouth. Here, with a permanent population of chronic invalids, it is difficult to envisage a competent physician failing. But Lamson managed to achieve this, due largely to his strange behaviour and to the development of what seems to have been a persecution mania. One of his servants was to describe later how the doctor would frequently fire a revolver out of the bedroom window, swearing that the Turks were massing down the road ready to attack the house!

Lamson soon sold this practice for far less than he had paid for it, and by this time his finances were at an extremely low ebb. He resolved to go to America, where he had several relatives, and with financial help from his wife managed to cross the Atlantic early in 1881. He was disappointed by what he found and after only a fortnight decided to return home. On the voyage back he introduced himself to the ship's doctor and volunteered to help in the sick bay. He also admitted he was very short of cash and borrowed £5. Needless to say the sum was never repaid. He was still living in Bournemouth, though he had sold the practice, but when he returned from America in April 1881 he found a considerable number of writs against him. The bank had foreclosed on his mortgage and his wife and child were forced to stay with Margaret and her husband.

In August 1881 the doctor announced to his relatives that he would be visiting America once again, for reasons never divulged. It so happened that his mother lived in Ventnor, on the Isle of Wight, and in August of that year Lamson, together with his wife and child, visited her for a week. At the same time Margaret and her husband, together with young Percy, were also due on holiday not far away at Shanklin.

When the Chapmans and Percy arrived at Shanklin station they were met by Lamson and Kate, who conducted them to Clarence Villa, the lodgings run by a Mrs Jolliffe. Before going to the station the doctor had called on a pharmacist in Ventnor High Street and presented a prescription which included one grain of the powerful vegetable poison aconitine, and some quinine sulphate powder.

Two days later he called again at Clarence Villa, stayed to tea and told his relatives that he could not remain long as he was off to America that night and had to leave very soon. During the course of the meal he commented that Percy did not seem very well, and gave him what he said was a quinine powder to improve his condition. He then left Clarence Villa en route for Southampton, from where he was due to sail for America.

After Lamson's departure Percy and the Chapmans read and talked until about 9.30 p.m., at which point Percy said he was not feeling very well and went to bed. An hour later his sister, Mrs Chapman, looked in on him, and Percy said he was feeling much worse, and described himself as being 'paralysed all over'. Both Mrs Jolliffe and Mrs Chapman took turns to peep into his room during the night, and on one of these occasions found Percy vomiting and obviously in great distress. The next morning he seemed a good deal better, ate a reasonable breakfast, and remained well for the remainder of the holiday except, of course, for his chronic disability.

On 24th October 1881 Lamson returned from his second visit to America, and went to London to stay at Nelson's Hotel. At this period he seems to have been virtually penniless, uttering cheques that were worthless and drawn on a bank where his account had already been closed, pawning his watch and selling several pieces of medical equipment, including a valuable case of surgical instruments, for comparatively small amounts.

On 30th November he decided to visit his mother again, but was unable to pay his fare from Ryde to Ventnor. The authorities allowed him to travel, however, as he said he had relatives on the Island who would reimburse the railway company. In Ventnor he went to see a friend, Price Owen, and cashed a cheque with him for £20 drawn on the Wilts and Dorset Bank. Having done this he immediately returned to London, and then sent Mr Owen a telegram asking him not to present the cheque, as he had inadvertently drawn it on the wrong bank. He said he would explain what had happened more fully later.

This, in fact, was a complete fabrication. It was true that he had no account with the Wilts and Dorset Bank for the very good reason that he was seriously overdrawn and the bank had closed it. He had no account with any other bank and the ploy was obviously designed to stop Owen presenting the cheque for as long as possible.

Back in London he embarked on an even more risky manoeuvre, drawing a cheque on a bank where he had never *had* an account. After being refused payment by various tradesmen he finally enlisted the assistance of a friend, John Tulloch, a medical student, who succeeded in getting a cheque cashed for him at the Eyre Arms, a pub in St John's Wood.

With hindsight it seems that his plans had gone badly astray, and it is highly probable that he had attempted to murder Percy John during the holidays on the Isle of Wight, for by Percy's death his wife would inherit a further £1,500 from the boy's estate. It has also been suggested that Lamson was responsible for the unexpected death of his other brother-in-law, Henry, which had taken place soon after his marriage to Kate and by which she had inherited £700. This, however, seems unlikely, and far less credible than the rather suspicious nature of the events which took place at Shanklin, events which were to be used so dramatically against the doctor at his eventual trial.

Now Lamson had one last desperate effort to make. He would have to risk another attempt on the life of Percy John, and this time there could be no mistake. The doctor laid his plans with the greatest care.

Despite his physical disabilities Percy John was a cheerful lad and exceptionally fond of his two sisters, with whom he often spent the holidays. He had been a cripple from birth, in addition suffering from ankylosing spondylitis, a painful affliction of the vertebrae of the spine associated with rheumatoid arthritis and producing a permanent curvature likely to increase as time goes by. Because of the paralysis of his lower limbs his life was spent almost entirely in a wheel-chair, and he was carried up and down stairs by other pupils at the school.

Percy also seemed very fond of his brother-in-law, George Lamson. Indeed, he tended to hero-worship him, and for a cripple doomed to a life of inactivity, Lamson's tales of the seige of Paris and his colourful adventures in the Balkans must have seemed particularly glamorous to Percy.

In 1881 he was eighteen years old and had been a resident of Blenheim School, Wimbledon, since he was fifteen. This was a private school owned by the headmaster, Mr William Bedbrook. He was subsequently to confirm that Percy was a popular pupil, cheerful most of the time, although occasionally given to bouts of depression when he could not join in the normal sports activities of the school.

75

On 2nd December 1881 Percey received the following letter from Lamson, written the previous day from Nelson's Hotel.

1st December 1881

My Dear Percy,

I had intended running down to Wimbledon to see you today, but I have been delayed by various matters until it is now nearly six o'clock, and by the time I should reach Blenheim House you would probably be preparing for bed. I leave for Florence and Paris tomorrow, and wish to see you before going. So I propose to run down to your place as early as I can, for a few minutes even, if I can accomplish no more. Believe me, dear boy, your loving brother.

G. H. Lamson.

In the event, a rather odd thing happened in connection with the promised visit. Lamson went to Wimbledon on the evening of 2nd December and arrived at the station in company with John Tulloch, the medical student who had assisted him in cashing his cheque at the Eyre Arms. They parted at the station and did not meet again until the next day. But Lamson did not visit Blenheim House that evening; what he did and where he spent the night remains a mystery. Despite this, the next day he told Tulloch that he had seen Percy, and that he was worried about his brother-in-law who, he said, was looking more and more ill each time he saw him.

The reason Lamson gave for not travelling to Paris that night was that he had spoken to Mr Bedbrook, who happened to be a Director of the South Eastern Railway Company. The Headmaster had advised him not to make the Channel crossing as the weather was stormy and there was 'a bad boat' running. This was, of course, a complete fabrication as Mr Bedbrook was not connected in any way with the South Eastern Railway Company and was certainly in no position to advise on the seaworthiness of cross-Channel steamers. In any case, Lamson had not visited the school nor seen Mr Bedbrook that night.

It was the following evening, 3rd December, that Lamson actually presented himself at the school shortly before 7 p.m. and asked to see Percy. That morning Percy had been carried downstairs as usual, had eaten his normal meals and at the time of Lamson's arrival was in the basement checking over some examination papers with another pupil. He was carried up to the first floor where he found his brother-in-law in conversation with Mr Bedbrook. The Headmaster was later to say how pale and thin Lamson was looking since he had last seen him.

The doctor greeted Percy with the words 'How fat you are looking, Percy, old boy' to which Percy replied 'I wish I could say the same of you, George.' After a few minutes of general conversation, Mr Bedbrook ordered sherry to be brought in, knowing Lamson's fondness for it. Lamson asked if he could have some sugar to take with the drink as this counteracted the effect of alcohol. Bedbrook was somewhat surprised, believing the reverse to be true, but none the less rang for the sugar which was brought in by Mrs Bowles, the matron, and placed on the table. The doctor put a teaspoonful of the castor sugar into his wine. He then produced three slices of fruit cake from a small black bag. He gave one piece each to Bedbrook and Percy and ate the remaining piece himself. Diving into his bag once more, he pulled out a box of empty gelatine capsules manufactured by the American pharmaceutical company of Parke, Davis and Co., and not yet available in Britain.

He said to Mr Bedbrook, 'While in America I did not forget you and your boys. I thought what excellent things these capsules would be for your boys to take nauseous medicines in.' While Bedbrook was examining the capsules, Lamson took one from the box, opened it, and filled it with sugar from the bowl. He explained that the capsule should be shaken after filling, to ensure the contents were evenly distributed, and then handed it to his brother-in-law: 'Percy, you are a champion pill-taker, take this. Show Mr Bedbrook how easy it is to swallow.'

Percy obediently swallowed the capsule.

The time by then was 7.15 p.m. and Lamson immediately rose and said he must catch the next train from Wimbledon to London Bridge, as he was travelling to Florence via Paris later that night. Mr Bedbrook pointed out that he had insufficient time to catch the 7.21 from Wimbledon, but that there was another train at 7.51. Although this gave him time to spare, for Blenheim House was not far from the station, the doctor left the school immediately.

Mr Bedbrook accompanied him to the door and Lamson remarked that Percy's curvature of the spine was more pronounced and that he did not think he would last long. Mr Bedbrook said nothing to this remark, though in his private opinion Percy was in very good health, apart from his permanent disability, and had had to have medical attention (for a skin complaint) only once in the three years he had been at the school.

It so happened that Mr Bedbrook was entertaining guests at the school that evening. After Lamson's somewhat hurried departure he went back to where he had left Percy before he rejoined his friends. He found Percy looking rather sorry for himself, and when Bedbrook asked if anything was wrong the boy said he felt ill and seemed to be having a severe bout of heartburn.

Mr Bedbrook returned to the party, listened to two young ladies singing duets at the piano, and then returned to see Percy once more. This time he was much worse and said to Mr Bedbrook, 'I feel as I felt after my brother-in-law gave me a quinine powder at Shanklin in the summer.'

The Headmaster arranged for Percy to be carried upstairs to his room, but no more than an hour later he was called by Mrs Bowles and Mr Godward, a junior master who was particularly fond of Percy. This time the boy was obviously in great pain, throwing himself about the bed and vomiting copiously. At times it took their united efforts to hold him down.

One of the guests at the party was a physician, Dr Other William Berry, who was also the official medical officer of the school and who knew Percy well. To him Percy managed to convey the information that he had severe stomach pains and that his throat felt as if it were contracting and that he could not swallow. Dr Berry asked him if he had ever felt like that before, and Percy repeated his statement about being given a powder by Lamson at Shanklin.

Dr Berry arranged for hot poultices to be applied to Percy's stomach and told Mrs Bowles to give him a beaten-up white of egg. This had no effect and Dr Berry decided to give Percy an injection of morphine to ease the pain. This brought only a temporary relief, and at 11 p.m. another injection of morphine was administered. Soon after this Percy lapsed into a coma and at about twenty past eleven he died.

Dr Berry could find no natural cause for the death of his patient, but was convinced that he had died through the ingestion of some powerful irritant vegetable poison. The party was long over, and an uneasy peace descended on Blenheim House for the remainder of that night.

The following morning Mr Bedbrook decided to inform the police of the suspicious circumstances surrounding the death of Percy John. The enquiries were placed in the hands of Inspector Fuller, who later that day visited the school and collected various items including the castor sugar and a box of quinine powders the doctor had sent to Percy labelled

'J. Littlefield, chemist, Ventnor'. He also took the remainder of the decanter of sherry and some Dundee cake.

As a result of Inspector Fuller's report, a post-mortem was conducted by Dr Berry and another Wimbledon doctor, assisted by Dr Thomas Bond, Lecturer in Forensic Medicine at the Westminster Hospital. These gentlemen could find no direct cause for the death of the boy, nor was anything suspicious found in the sugar, cake or sherry. On the instructions of the Home Secretary, a further and more extensive autopsy was performed by Dr Thomas Stevenson. He was a Home Office analyst, Professor of Medical Jurisprudence at Guy's Hospital, and one of the most eminent toxicologists in Europe. Stevenson found grey patches on the stomach lining indicative of gross irritation and causing intense pain. In his opinion death was due to a vegetable alkaloid such as aconitine administered shortly before death. A small quantity of aconitine had been found in a raisin extracted from the digestive organs. There was also something odd about the quinine powders from the Ventnor pharmacist. They consisted of twenty packets of powder, six large and fourteen small, all in one box. On analysis all except one contained pure and unadulterated quinine sulphate powder. The sole exception was one of the small powders, which contained quinine and also one grain of aconitine, a lethal dose if taken internally.

The first newspaper report of the death of Percy John and the circumstances surrounding the matter appeared in the *Daily Telegraph* on 5th December 1881 under the headline 'Mysterious Death of Wimbledon Student'.

The report continued:

It is understood that the police authorities are in possession of some strange details relative to the death of Mr Percy Malcolm John, aged nineteen, a student at Blenheim School, Wimbledon, which occurred on Saturday night.

Mr John was the sole surviving heir of considerable property, and it is not known how long his mother and father have been dead. He has two sisters, one of whom is the wife of a Dr Lamson, but none of them have a settled residence in England.

Dr Lamson called at the school on Saturday evening and saw his brother-in-law in company with Mr William Henry Bedbrook, the principal of the establishment. The visit did not last altogether twenty minutes, and soon after Dr Lamson had left the deceased began to feel ill. He said at first that he suffered somewhat in the way he did when he took a quinine pill on the Isle of Wight.

He gradually grew worse, and then commenced to vomit, complaining all the time of a burning sensation at the heart, while his lower limbs were paralysed. Medical aid was called at once. Fortunately Mr Berry, a surgeon, was at Blenheim House School at the time, and he was called upstairs as soon as the unfavourable symptoms began to present themselves. At the same time Dr Little was sent for, and both gentlemen remained with Mr Malcolm John (*sic*: Malcolm was his second name) until he died in great agony at half-past eleven o'clock the same night.

Before his death the deceased made a statement which has caused grave suspicions.

The coroner for the western district of Surrey, Mr. J.H. Hall of Kingston-on-Thames, has been communicated with, and will open an inquest on the body of the deceased today or tomorrow.

On enquiry having been made of the police at Scotland Yard, it was stated that an order had been made for an arrest, which was subsequently countermanded.

A newspaper report on the inquest proceedings held next day again mentioned Lamson by name, and also stated that death was almost certainly due to poisoning by aconitine or

81

a similar vegetable alkaloid. This report was read by a dispensing assistant employed by Allen and Hanbury's, of Plough Court in the City of London, who remembered selling a quantity of aconitine to a doctor called Lamson on 24th November. After consultation with his colleague, who had supervised the sale and checked Lamson's name in the Medical Directory, the two assistants informed the manager, who at once communicated with the police.

But what of Lamson himself since the death of Percy on 3rd December?

After leaving Blenheim House he had returned to London by train and had later caught the night boat-train from London Bridge, crossed to France via Dover and Calais and arrived in Paris the next afternoon. There he presumably stayed with friends, for he had little money, but on 7th December he read in an English newspaper that his name was being mentioned in connection with Percy John's death. Earlier he had received a letter from his brother-in-law, William Chapman, advising him of Percy's death, and Lamson wrote back immediately as follows:

Paris, Wednesday Morning,
7th December 1881

My Dear Will,

Your letter reached me on Monday night too late to catch any train except one, via Dieppe, and which I should have had to rush for. This the doctor would not allow me to do. I was so prostrate at the sudden, awful and unexpected news that I became delirious very soon. I was obliged to remain in bed all day yesterday. Early this morning I saw the *Evening Standard*. I read therein the dreadful suspicion attached to my name. I need not tell you of the absolute falsity of such an accusation. Bedbrook was present all the time I was in the house, and if there was any noxious substance in the capsule it must have been in his sugar, for that is all there was in it. He saw me take the empty capsule and fill it from his own sugar basin. However, with the consciousness that I am an innocent and unjustly accused man, I am returning at once to London to face the matter out. I shall attempt no concealment. If they wish to arrest me they will have ample opportunity of doing so. I shall arrive at Waterloo Station about 9.15 tomorrow (Thursday) morning. Do try and meet me there. If I do not see you there I shall go straight to your house, trusting the possibility of finding Kitty there. In great haste, yours truly,

Geo. H. Lamson

W.G. Chapman, Esq.

Lamson then set out for London, crossing the Channel via Le Havre and Southampton. He arrived at Waterloo, where he met Chapman as arranged. They then went to Chapman's house, and from there, accompanied by his wife Kate, the doctor made the journey to Scotland Yard.

They were received by Inspector Butcher, who was in charge of the investigations. Lamson explained that he had been in Paris when he had been told of Percy's death, and after reading the newspaper report had decided to come home immediately and offer the police all the help he could.

Inspector Butcher listened attentively. When Lamson had finished he asked him to remain a while so that he could consult his superiors. He was away some time, to the intense annoyance of Lamson, who told another policeman present that he was on his way with his wife to spend the week-end at Chichester, and that he had intended only to leave a forwarding address with the police should they wish to interview him at a later date. Eventually Butcher returned with a high-ranking officer, and to his dismay Lamson heard that he was under arrest.

Butcher said to him, 'Your case has been fully considered, and it has been decided to charge you with causing the death of Percy John. I thereupon take you into custody, and charge you with causing the death of Percy Malcolm John at Blenheim House, Wimbledon, on 3rd December.'

Lamson seemed stunned. His first question was 'Do you think bail will be accepted?' He then said that he hoped things would be kept as quiet as possible 'for the sake of my relations'. The Inspector told him that he would be taken to Wandsworth Prison and would then appear before the Wandsworth magistrates, who would decide the question of bail. In the event bail was refused, and Lamson then appeared in court for the first time at Bow Street, where the committal proceedings took place on 30th December. After various remands in custody he was committed for trial at the Central Criminal Court.

Kate Lamson, still staying with her sister Margaret and her family, steadfastly refused to believe that her husband could possibly be guilty of causing the death of her young brother. Her belief was shared by the remainder of the family, including Lamson's mother, and, indeed, it is a feature of many murder cases that those nearest to the perpetrator of the crime have the least inkling of his true character. Time and time again murderers are described by those nearest them as 'kind' and 'gentle' or 'unwilling to hurt a fly' and though Lamson was known to be eccentric, no member of his own family believed in his guilt. Mrs Lamson's unwavering loyalty to her husband from the moment of his arrest to his appearance in the dock was a factor of which much was made by Lamson's counsel.

The trial of George Henry Lamson began at the Old Bailey, London, on Wednesday, 8th March 1882 and lasted six days. According to newspaper reports of the time the affair aroused great interest and the court was crowded to suffocation, with an even larger crowd waiting outside. The public galleries were full to over-flowing, reporters from almost every national newspaper crammed the press-box and the police were everywhere.

The judge was Sir Henry Hawkins and even the bench seemed to be crowded, for sitting with him were several City of London Aldermen and magistrates. They were there purely as spectators however, and took no part in the proceedings.

The prosecution was in the hands of the Solicitor-General, Sir Farrer Herschell, and Lamson was defended by Mr Montagu Williams, Q.C., leading Mr Charles Mathews and Mr W. S. Robson and instructed by Mr A. H. Mills, solicitor.

At 10.45 the prisoner was brought up from the cells below. An eye-witness at the trial described him as

' . . . apparently a highly intelligent man, with a pallid face, piercing dark brown eyes, not cruel, but rather tender and profound, moustache, whiskers and a slight beard; beneath his eyes were dark rims, speaking of wakeful nights and mental tension; though slightly nervous he was generally composed; his mouth was rather weak − it receded below somewhat; but his brow was a fine one, albeit deeply lined.'

The Solicitor-General first outlined the case against the prisoner as the prosecution saw it, dealing with Lamson's chronic shortage of money, the inheritance his wife would receive in the event of Percy John's death, his purchase and possession of aconitine, his visit to Wimbledon on 3rd December, Percy's death later that evening and Lamson's precipitate departure for Paris.

His first witness was William Bedbrook, whose evidence was chiefly concerned with the curious business of the ready-cut cake and the empty gelatine capsules. In his cross-examination, Mr Williams elicited the information that Percy had been taking exams the day prior to his death and that when the school closed for Christmas he had intended spending the holiday with his sister, Mrs Lamson.

A pupil at the school, Walter Banbury, described how he had carried Percy upstairs after he fell ill on that evening. He was followed in the box by Mrs Bowles, the school matron. This lady was a most unreliable witness, and at first denied having seen Percy John at all on 3rd December. She later corrected herself, saying that she had got the dates muddled. She described fetching the castor sugar and subsequently seeing Percy in great pain upstairs in his room. In cross-examination she made the curious remark that it was she who had asked Percy if he had felt as bad as that when he was at Shanklin, to which Percy had replied 'No'. Mr Williams also asked about the kind of medicine the boys were given at school and about some experiments Percy had been doing with a chemistry set.

An important witness was Dr Berry, who had ministered to Percy during his last hours. He described the results of the post-mortem examination, and said that in his opinion death was due to aconitine or some vegetable poison akin to it. In cross-examination he admitted that he knew very little about the drug and its action, had never seen a case of poisoning by aconitine and was even unaware that it was listed in the *British Pharmocopoeia*. He also said that he knew of aconitine being used in an ointment to relieve the pain of rheumatism but had never prescribed any for Percy. He described collecting some of Percy's vomit for analysis and confirmed that he had given the boy two injections of morphine during the evening to ease his pain.

During the next five days a total of fifty-four witnesses entered and left the box. They included the two assistants at the Plough Court pharmacy who had sold aconitine to Lamson in November. They had supplied him with the drug merely on his statement that he was Dr George Henry Lamson and that a doctor of this name appeared in the

Medical Directory. On this admission the judge was somewhat critical, pointing out that apparently anyone could choose a name from the Medical Directory, pass himself off as that person and so obtain poisons illegally. In mitigation of his action one assistant, Dodd, said that Lamson had appeared to be well-dressed and of generally respectable appearance, but the main proof that he was a genuine doctor, in his view, was that his writing was almost illegible!

By far the most important witness was Dr Thomas Stevenson, the Home Office pathologist and toxicologist and an 'expert' witness in the mould of Swaine Taylor before him and Sir Bernard Spilsbury in years to come. He described in full the analysis of the contents of Percy's stomach, and gave details of the manner in which the material had been washed, digested with alcohol, precipitated again with other chemicals, finally ending as an oily substance which contained the fatal drug. This residue of the stomach contents had been injected into mice, who promptly died, apparently in great agony, and Stevenson and his assistants had made the final test by placing the material on their tongues. Stevenson was convinced that the residue contained aconitine and that there was no doubt this had caused the death of Percy.

The defence had one strong card to play. Nobody, not even the 'expert' Dr Stevenson, had ever seen a case of human poisoning by aconitine sufficient to cause death. How could he be sure it was present in Percy's body, and even if it were present, how could he be sure it was the cause of death? Stevenson would not be shifted. He knew the action of aconitine — indeed, he was a world authority on the subject, and in his view there was no shadow of doubt that Percy had died of it. Mr Montagu Williams did not pursue the matter.

After Dr Stevenson there remained only a few minor witnesses such as John Tulloch, the medical student, with his evidence of helping Lamson to cash a cheque and Mr Nelson, proprietor of Nelson's Hotel in Great Portland Street, who confirmed that Lamson was in financial trouble. A pawnbroker told of Lamson pledging many of his possessions and another man told of buying the case of surgical instruments from Lamson for a very small sum.

By the afternoon of the fifth day of the trial the prosecution had completed its case and there was a short break before Montagu Williams began his speech for the defence.

He called no witnesses, and could not put Lamson in the box since the right of a prisoner to give evidence on his own behalf was not granted until 1898. Mr Williams relied for his defence on the fact that aconitine was a little-known poison and that 'the evidence of the scientific witnesses for the prosecution consists solely of theories'.

He was scathing about the complex chemical tests undertaken to establish the presence of the poison in Percy's stomach, and suggested that after so many reactions from so many chemicals the final product may have been changed considerably from its original form. The fact that it killed mice when injected into them proved nothing, for it was known that mice died easily from shock, which, in this case, could have been produced by the prick of the needle.

He made much of the fact that Percy had intended spending the Christmas holidays with his sister, Mrs Lamson, and said that if the doctor had really intended poisoning his brother-in-law he could have done so with far less fear of detection in family surroundings. He refused to believe that aconitine was introduced into the capsule of sugar, for had not Mr Bedbrook seen quite clearly the capsule filled with sugar from the basin, and nothing else added?

Finally he reminded the jury that Lamson was a highly intelligent man, and certainly would not have acted in such a suspicious manner had he really been intent on murder. In particular, he would never have returned voluntarily from

France on hearing of Percy's death. That was not the action of a guilty man.

Before closing, Williams drew the attention of the jury to the presence of the prisoner's wife in court. She had been a constant source of strength and inspiration to him since the terrible day of his arrest at Scotland Yard and believed absolutely in his innocence. What would happen to her and their child if he were convicted? In a fine flight of rhetoric directed purposefully at the jury, Williams said, 'What a reward for all her true nobility — a widowed home, a cursed life and a little child never to be taught to lisp its father's name, its inheritance of Cain!' The jury, it is said, remained singularly unmoved.

The Solicitor-General, in his final speech, was on firmer ground. He said he was quite satisfied by the medical evidence that aconitine had been the cause of Percy's death. This being so, who could have administered it except Lamson, who was known to have had the poison in his possession shortly before? Motive there was in plenty, and it had been proved that Lamson had been in great financial straits. His sudden departure from Wimbledon on the night in question was an exact parallel to his action in leaving Shanklin, for on both occasions he had attempted to put as much distance as possible between himself and Percy. The fact that he had returned from France of his own volition proved nothing. When searched at Scotland Yard he had in his possession only a few shillings and seven francs. He could not have remained in Paris any longer, and had not the means to travel further afield.

The judge then summed up for the jury, and they retired. They took only thirty minutes to arrive at their verdict: guilty. Sir Henry Hawkins pronounced the sentence of death, and after being allowed a brief word with his wife the prisoner was taken to the cells.

In prison Lamson was visited by his wife and his father, a clergyman living in Florence, and wrote various letters to friends. In one of them he confessed to his crime, using the words: ' . . . under present conditions, and in my right and normal state of mind, the compassing and committing such a crime as that for which I must now die would have been utterly and absolutely impossible.' He also confessed to the prison chaplain.

The execution was fixed for 2nd April 1882 but was postponed until 18th April as a result of various representations from friends in America and England who wished to give affidavits about his character and state of mind. Many of these indicated that for some years Lamson's mind had been wandering, almost certainly due to his addiction to morphine, and that he was clearly not responsible for his actions. These matters had not been fully considered by 18th April, and the execution was postponed once more. Lamson finally went to the gallows on 28th April.

On 29th April the *Daily Telegraph* printed the following account of his execution and last hours:

Lamson awoke yesterday morning at an early hour, after having had a tolerably quiet night's rest. Soon after he rose the chaplain of the gaol entered the condemned cell, and from that moment forward, save during the interval of breakfast, the convict was engaged in devotional services. On the previous day the scaffold had been got ready, and consequently there was no noise to disturb the culprit as he ate or pursued his devotions. The drop used on two previous occasions had already been fitted together, and had been duly inspected by Marwood (the hangman) on the afternoon before. It is true that the executioner, on arriving at the gaol, had found the pit to be of an insufficient depth, and had directed that an additional 18 inches should be dug out, but this had occasioned no noise, and for several hours prior to the execution

Lamson heard nothing to distract his thoughts. The evening preceding had been spent by the culprit revising his private business, writing letters to friends, arranging monetary affairs and generally concluding whatever communications he desired to make with his relatives. Then came retirement and sleep.

About a quarter to nine o'clock the bell of the gaol began to toll, greatly disturbing the condemned man, who now learnt that his time had nearly come. Very shortly afterwards the Under-Sheriff, the deputy governor of the gaol, the surgeon, and four warders made their appearance in the cell, with a view to preparing the convict for his last act. At Wandsworth it seems they have a curious custom. Usually in other gaols it is the method to pinion the prisoner inside his cell, a mode both convenient and commendable. But, for reasons best known to themselves, the officials of this prison prefer to have this operation performed in the open air. Thus it happened that Lamson, who had donned the suit of black that he wore at his trial, was allowed to walk freely from his cell between two warders, at about five minutes to nine, in the direction of the scaffold. That structure chanced happily to be hidden from the point of view of the door by which the culprit had just emerged by a corner of the wall, so that at first he could not see it or the newly-dug grave. On the procession went, formed in the following order: — Two warders, bearing white wands; then the clergyman of the gaol, in surplice and hood; next the convict, supported by two warders, who at this period had no necessity to assist him in walking; and finally the deputy governor and the surgeon, with several more warders. Marwood, who just then was waiting within the inner gates, with his straps thrown over his arms only, hesitated until the cortège should reach him. As it happened, Lamson had not seen him, and apparently had not expected him, when the leading warder came up to the place where the executioner was. Then there was a sudden pause, for Marwood, with uplifted hand, had called out 'Halt!' and the procession had stopped. That word 'halt' told its tale on the prisoner. Realizing to the full his position for the first time, to all seeming, Lamson now staggered, and almost fell against one of the warders who supported him. His tremor was, indeed, terribly apparent, and it was a great question for a moment whether he would not fall. But the executioner at this instant came to his aid, and with the help of the warders kept him in an upright position. Not removing the collar which Lamson had put on, and only turning in the points which might presently stand in the way of the rope, Marwood began to pinion him. 'I hope you will not hurt me,' the convict murmured, half in fear and possibly in way of remonstrance. 'I'll do my best not to hurt you: I'll be as gentle as I can,' responded Marwood, and the work went on. Marwood's plan was here apparent. Lamson was a more powerfully built man than he appeared, weighing upwards of 11 stone 12 lbs, and the executioner, evidently fearing that his strength would operate somewhat against a sharp and quick fall, fastened back his shoulders in a manner which precluded all possibility of the culprit resisting the action of the drop. For this reason, then, Lamson was fastened by the strap somewhat more tightly than Lefoy, whose slimness of figure was comparatively light weight of ten stone only furnished no necessity for any such precaution.

When the convict was pinioned the procession moved on, the clergyman meanwhile reading the service of the Church appointed for the burial of the dead, the doomed man responding almost inaudibly to the words uttered by the chaplain. It was with great difficulty that he could now walk at all; indeed, it is now certain that had he not been supported by the warders who stood on either side of him, he would have fallen to the earth. Suddenly he came in sight of the gallows — a black structure, about 30 yards distant. The grave, newly-dug, was close at hand. The new and terrible spectacle here acted once more with painful effect upon the condemned man, for again he almost halted and fell. But the warders, never leaving hold of him, moved on, while Marwood came behind. At last the gallows was reached, and here the clergyman bade farewell to the prisoner, while Marwood began his preparations with the rope and beam above. With a view to meet any accretion of fear which might now befall the culprit, a wise provision had been made. The drop was so arranged as to part in the middle, after the fashion of two folding doors; but, lest the doomed man might not be able to stand upon the scaffold without assistance, two planks of deal had been placed over the drop, one on either side of the rope, so that at the last moment the two warders supporting the convict might stand securely and hold him up, without danger to themselves or inconvenience to the machinery of the gallows. In this way Lamson was now kept erect while Marwood fastened his legs and put the cap over his eyes. He must have fallen had the arrangements been otherwise, for his efforts to appear composed had by this time failed. Indeed, from what now occurred it is evident that the convict yet hoped for a few more minutes of life, for, as Marwood proceeded to pull the cap over his face, he pitifully begged that one more prayer be recited by the chaplain. Willing as the executioner possibly might have been to listen to this request, he had, of course, no power to alter the progress of the service, and was obliged to disregard this last request of the dying man. Signalling the warders to withdraw their arms, he drew the lever, which released the bolt under the drop, and so launched the prisoner into eternity. The clergyman finished the Lord's Prayer, in the midst of which he found himself when the lever had been pulled, and then, pronouncing the benediction, moved slowly back to the prison. Of course the body hung in its place for an hour, in accordance with the law, after which it was taken down and placed in a shell coffin for the purpose of inspection.

Though Lamson confessed to poisoning Percy, oddly enough the way the poison was administered was never established in court. It seems most likely that it was present in a previously-selected slice of the fruit cake; the post-mortem had revealed a raisin impregnated with aconitine. This damning piece of evidence, though mentioned by the prosecution at the trial, was never pursued, even though it would probably have established just how the poison was administered to the victim. Lamson almost certainly used the capsule and the castor sugar as a blind to confuse the police. He apparently succeeded. But there was plenty of evidence to convict him without the poisoned raisin, and Lamson died alone and afraid on the gallows at Wandsworth Prison.

5

Thomas Neill Cream

(1850-1892)

The mind of the mass murderer obviously works in a very mysterious and unpredictable way. Thomas Neill Cream was a multiple murderer, and from an early age had exhibited a precocity of behaviour remarkable for his years and which soon brought him to the notice of the police.

Though murder is the most serious of all crimes, many murderers are found to have led blameless lives up to the moment of the actual killing. This leads to the odd situation that a man charged with murder can also be classified as a first offender — something which may cause problems to the prison authorities when a suspected murderer is on remand awaiting trial.

Neill Cream had not, however, led a blameless life. Though the seriousness of his youthful escapades was not brought home to him, they represented the beginning of a life of crime which was to end in one of the most sensational trials of the century. He is also one of the few men to have been convicted of murder and to have lived to commit several more.

Cream was born in Glasgow in 1850, the first of a family of eight children. When he was five years old his father decided to emigrate to Canada and in 1855 the family settled in Quebec where Cream senior was appointed manager of a lumber firm. The pay was good, and despite the arrival of more and more children, the Creams were able to live in a style to which they had been totally unaccustomed in Glasgow.

Young Thomas was first apprenticed to his father's firm, but his extreme intelligence seemed to make him worthy of higher things. Mainly through the insistence of his mother he was registered at McGill University, Montreal, in 1869 to read medicine, and in the spring of 1876 he qualified as a doctor.

Even during his student days his activities warranted suspicion, particularly in respect of two attempts to claim large sums in insurance as the result of mysterious fires at his home and at his lodgings. He was suspected of both fraud and arson but was quick-witted enough to avoid any charges.

The year that he qualified was clouded by the affair of Flora Brooks, whom he had met when she was visiting Montreal. An affair developed between Cream and Flora and a few months later she discovered she was pregnant. She underwent an abortion, almost certainly at the hands of her lover, and, though getting rid of the child, nearly died as a result. Flora's father sought out Cream and insisted that he marry his daughter. This he did in September 1876, with noticeable reluctance, but immediately left for England on the pretext of continuing his medical studies at St Thomas's Hospital in London.

Flora Brooks never recovered from her traumatic experience, and died in August of the following year. Cream was informed, and wrote from London expressing his sorrow and, at the same time, claiming $1,000 under the marriage contract. After some argument he was eventually pleased to accept $200.

Later in 1877 Cream returned to Canada and bought himself a practice in London, Ontario. Very soon afterwards the body of a young girl was found mysteriously amongst the dustbins at the rear of Cream's surgery. A half-empty bottle of chloroform was nearby, and it was subsequently proved that she could not have taken this herself. At the inquest friends of the dead girl gave evidence that she had been pregnant, and had been visiting Cream to arrange an abortion. At the same time a wealthy local businessman, who knew the girl, had received a letter from an anonymous source accusing him of having seduced the girl and demanding a large sum in 'hush money'. Though the whole affair was highly suspect, it was never proved that Cream had caused the death by an illegal abortion, nor that he had attempted to blackmail the businessman. Nevertheless enough suspicion was attached to Cream for it to ruin his practice and force him to move to Chicago.

In Chicago he once again demonstrated this extraordinary propensity for having young girls die in or around his surgery. In 1880 he was arrested after Julia Faulkner died on the premises in the course of undergoing an abortion. But once again the evidence was inconclusive and the case was dropped. A few months later another female patient died at her home as the result of an overdose of drugs given by Cream. During the investigations into this affair Cream tried to blackmail the local druggist, Frank Pyatt, by saying that the medicine he had given the girl had been incorrectly dispensed. Pyatt passed the letter on to the police, who were by then increasingly interested in everything Cream did, but before any action could be taken the sinister doctor was caught up in the affair of Daniel Stott and his wife, which nearly cost him his life.

Stott was an epileptic and, with his blonde wife Mabel, lived in the Chicago suburb of Garden Prairie. Stott was sixty and his wife thirty-three, and the couple began visiting Cream in response to his advertisement in the local paper claiming to cure epilepsy by hypnotism. After a few visits to the surgery, Mabel Stott found it convenient to leave her husband at home and see Cream on her own, ostensibly to obtain supplies of a medication that would enhance the effect of the hypnosis.

A passionate affair developed between doctor and patient's wife. Stott's condition deteriorated and nobody was particularly surprised when he died in June 1881. What did surprise everyone, however, was that on Stott's death Mabel and Cream immediately eloped to Canada. Once in Canada he did a quite extraordinary thing: he wrote to the coroner of the district in which the Stotts had lived suggesting that Daniel's body be exhumed and tested for strychnine! Once again he suggested that the dispensing of Frank Pyatt was at fault. The body was exhumed and strychnine found.

Unfortunately for Cream, Mabel Stott had by then become disillusioned with her lover and also thoroughly frightened. She, in turn, wrote to the police saying that she had been present when Cream himself had added a quantity of white powder to her husband's medicine after attempting to insure his life. The pair were immediately arrested in Canada and brought back to stand trial in Chicago. Mrs Stott was acquitted and vanished from the scene, but Cream was convicted of murder in the second degree, surprisingly, and sentenced to imprisonment for life.

He began his prison sentence in September 1881, but, inexplicably, this was later commuted to a term of seventeen years. With remission for good conduct he actually served only ten years and was released in July 1891. By then he was a rich man, for his father had died and left him a fortune of $16,000 in Canadian stock. On leaving prison he returned to Canada, made the necessary financial arrangements, and decided to go to England. He arrived at Liverpool on the S.S. *Teutonic* on 1st October and a few days later travelled to London.

Cream's career to date had demonstrated that he was a thoroughly evil man. He was also a very clever one, and his only appearance in court, on the murder charge, was almost entirely due to his own action in communicating with the coroner. Here we see the first manifestation of that abnormal conceit that is the hallmark of so many multiple murderers, in that they cannot bear to think that their expertise is going unrecognized, and purposely draw attention to their crimes in the supreme conviction that they are too clever ever to pay the penalty. Cream's later actions in England prove this point only too well.

Arriving in London on 5th October 1891 he booked in at Anderson's Hotel in Fleet Street. Exploring the neighbourhood the next evening, he met a prostitute called Eliza Masters and took her for a drink at the King Lud, a large public house at the bottom of Ludgate Hill. From there they went to Gatti's Music-Hall in the Strand, where they met a friend of Masters called Eliza May in the bar. These two girls shared lodgings in the area of the Lambeth Road, and before leaving them that evening Cream said he would write and make another date with them.

On the 9th October Masters received a letter from Cream saying that he would call that afternoon between 2 p.m. and 5 p.m. The two Elizas sat in the window looking out for him, and about four o'clock Cream appeared. Before he reached the house, and much to the fury of the girls, the doctor was accosted by another prostitute called Matilda Clover and went off with her. They followed the pair to Clover's lodgings, but neither Cream nor the girl reappeared that evening and Masters and May returned home in disgust.

Between arriving in London and writing to Masters, the doctor had not been idle. He had moved from the hotel in Fleet Street to lodgings run by a Mrs Sleaper in Lambeth Palace Road, and had also visited an optician in the Strand, had an eye-test, and ordered two pairs of spectacles intended to remove a pronounced squint. From a pharmacy in Westminster he had also bought a quantity of tincture of nux vomica, the active ingredient of which is strychnine, saying that he needed it for medical studies at St Thomas's

Hospital. He had also bought some large empty gelatine capsules, but had later changed them for smaller ones, more easily swallowed.

On the evening of 13th October a prostitute named Ellen Donworth was found lying on the pavement near the York Hotel in the Waterloo Road. She was obviously in very great agony, suffering from what were afterwards described as tetanic convulsions. A doctor was called, who ordered her immediate removal to hospital, but she died on the way. Before she died she was able to tell her listeners that 'a tall, dark man with cross eyes, a silk hat and bushy whiskers gave me a drink twice out of a bottle with white stuff in it.'

Naturally, there was an inquest and a post-mortem, at which it was found that Ellen's death had been caused by the ingestion of a large quantity of strychnine. During the course of the inquest, the coroner was handed a note that had just been delivered, which read as follows:

London, 19th October 1891.

To G. P. Wyatt Esq.
Deputy Coroner,
East Surrey.

I am writing to say that if you and your satellites fail to bring the murderer of Ellen Donworth, alias Ellen Linnell, late of 8 Duke Street, Westminster Bridge Road, to justice, that I am willing to give such assistance as will bring the murderer to justice, provided your Government is willing to pay £300,000 for my services. No pay if not successful.

A. O'Brien, Detective.

The Coroner, reading this extraordinary letter, decided it was the work of a madman and handed it over to Scotland

Yard. Three days later Mr Frederick Smith, Managing Director of the famous stationery firm of W.H. Smith & Co., received a letter in the same hand accusing him of murdering Ellen Donworth, but offering to 'get him off' on payment of a similar amount. This time the letter was signed 'H. Bayne, Barrister'. The writer said that if the terms were acceptable a note addressed to 'H. Bayne' should be exhibited in the window of the company's shop in the Strand. In accordance with police instructions this was done, but the mysterious writer never showed himself. Both this letter and the one to the coroner were later proved to have been written by Cream himself.

It will be remembered that on 9th October Masters and May, the two prostitutes, had seen Cream being waylaid by Matilda Clover and had followed the couple to her house. The maid employed by Clover's landlady was a pert young girl called Lucy Rose who was particularly interested in the sexual adventures of her mistress's lodger. So interested was she that she was not averse to reading any letters Matilda was careless enough to leave about and on 11th October, while cleaning the room, she found and read a letter to Matilda from somebody signed 'Fred', saying he would call on her the following night. Fred specially requested that Matilda should either destroy the letter or return it to him when he arrived.

Though this letter was never found, Lucy Rose had a retentive memory, and when the time came was able to repeat it to the police word for word. She also had a good look at 'Fred' when he duly arrived the following night, and the description she gave matched that already supplied by the luckless Ellen Donworth.

Matilda Clover was well on the way to being an alcoholic, and when, a few hours after 'Fred's' departure, she began screaming and shouting in pain, her landlady assumed that she was suffering from a bout of D.T.s. Lucy Rose went to see Matilda, and found her lying across the bed in great agony, unclothed, with her head fixed between the bedstead and the wall. In a lucid moment she cried, 'That man Fred has poisoned me — he gave me some pills.' It is of significance that Cream was known as 'Fred' to all the girls, and none knew his correct identity.

The landlady decided to call a doctor. When he arrived and examined the girl he, too, was of the opinion that she was suffering from delirium tremens brought about by alcoholic poisoning. The wretched Matilda died while the doctor was attending her, and he signed a death certificate giving excessive intake of alcohol as the cause of death. Matilda Clover was buried in Tooting Cemetery on 20th October.

About a month later, on 30th November, a highly respected physician named Dr William Broadbent received the following letter:

London, 28th November 1891

Sir,

Miss Clover, who, until a short time ago, lived at 27 Lambeth Palace Road, S.E., died at the above address on 20th October (last month) through being poisoned with strychnine. After her death a search of her effects was made, and evidence was found which showed that you not only gave her the medicine that caused her death, but that you had been hired for the purpose of poisoning her. This evidence is in the hands of one of our detectives, who will give the evidence either to you or to the police authorities for the sum of £2,500 (two thousand five hundred pounds sterling). You can have the evidence for £2,500 and in that way save yourself from ruin. If the matter is disposed of to the police it will be made public by being placed in the papers, and ruin you for ever. Now, sir, if you want the evidence for £2,500 just put a personal in the *Daily Chronicle* saying that you will pay Malone £2,500 for his services, and I will send a party to settle this matter just this − £2,500 sterling on the one hand and ruin, shame and disgrace on the other. Answer by personal on the first page of the *Daily Chronicle* any time next week. I am not humbugging you.

M. Malone

At that point there had been no post-mortem on Matilda Clover, whose death had been officially certified as due to alcoholic poisoning, and presumably the only person who knew she had died of strychnine was the person who gave it her. Dr Broadbent passed the letter on to Scotland Yard, where it joined the earlier letters from 'A. O'Brien' and 'H. Bayne'.

In the meantime the police arranged for a personal advertisement to be placed in the *Daily Chronicle* as instructed, but once again the writer did not come forward.

Christmas 1891 passed uneventfully, at least as far as the prostitute population was concerned, and on 7th January 1892 Dr Neill Cream returned to Canada for a spell, sailing on the S.S. *Sarnia* out of Liverpool. Two matters of some significance took place while he was in Canada, which had a direct bearing on later events in Britain.

First, he ordered a quantity of strychnine pills from a manufacturing chemist in New York, at the same time offering himself as their British representative. The company sent him the pills via their Canadian agent, but declined his offer of representation.

Secondly, while staying in a hotel in Quebec, he had 500 circulars printed addressed to guests at the Metropole Hotel in London.

The circular read as follows:

ELLEN DONWORTH'S DEATH

To the Guests
          of the Metropole Hotel

Ladies and Gentlemen,

   I hereby notify you that the person who poisoned
Ellen Donworth on the 14th last October is today in
the employee of the Metropole Hotel and that your lives
are in danger as long as you remain in this Hotel.

                    Yours respectfully

                                   W.H. Murray.

London, April 1892

The draft of the circular given to the printer was in Cream's
normal handwriting.

   Armed with this material, Cream returned to London on
2nd April, first staying at Edward's Hotel in Euston Square
but later returning to his original lodgings with Mrs Sleaper
in Lambeth Palace Road.

   A few weeks later there followed the murder of two young
women who had come from Brighton to London to work as
prostitutes and who lived in Stamford Street not far from
Cream's lodgings. A man answering to Cream's description
had been seen leaving their house late one evening, and a few
hours afterwards the girls, Alice Marsh and Emma Shrivell,
were found dying in agony in their bedrooms. In their last
moments both were able to describe how a tall, dark man
called Fred had had supper with them at their lodgings, and
had given to each of them a gelatine capsule purporting to be
a powerful aphrodisiac. The inquest on the victims, held at
St Thomas's Hospital, showed that death was due to
strychnine poisoning, though there was nothing to indicate
how it had been administered.

   Also living at Cream's lodgings was a young medical
student named Walter Harper. His father was a doctor in

Barnstaple, and the young man was of a quiet disposition and unlike the concept of the average medical student. A few days after the inquest on Marsh and Shrivell, Cream astounded his landlady by telling her that he had incontrovertible proof that young Harper had murdered the two prostitutes! Mrs Sleaper was highly indignant at this slur on her favourite lodger and told Cream he must be mad. She may have been nearer the truth than she realized.

On 26th April, in Barnstaple, Dr Harper received a letter, posted in London, saying that his son was undoubtedly the murderer of Marsh and Shrivell, but that the writer would be willing to suppress the evidence on payment of £1,500. The doctor handed the letter to the police and it eventually joined the other letters at the Yard. The doctor did not hear from the writer again.

By now the police were extremely concerned about this latest series of prostitute murders, and their inability to nail the culprit. It was, after all, less than four years since the bloody 'Jack the Ripper' atrocities in Whitechapel, and the police were still smarting at their failure to identify the murderer. Now it seemed a fresh, if less gory, spate of killings was beginning, and the police accordingly redoubled their efforts.

It so happened that about this time Cream made the acquaintance of a Sergeant McIntyre of the C.I.D. at Scotland Yard. They met socially through a mutual friend, and inevitably the conversation turned to the double murder and what was being talked about as 'The Lambeth Mystery'. Cream told the C.I.D. man that he had recently met another detective called Murray who had shown him a letter the two girls had received a few days prior to their murder. The letter, said Cream, warned the girls to be very wary of a young medical student called Harper, who would murder them 'as surely as he had murdered Matilda Clover and Lou Harvey'.

Though Sgt McIntyre knew about Matilda Clover, he had never heard the name of Lou Harvey and had no knowledge of anyone of that name being murdered. In the course of his enquiries he found that there was no detective called Murray in the Metropolitan Police Force or at Scotland Yard.

As a result, Sgt McIntyre became distinctly suspicious of Cream, in particular in connection with his intimate knowledge of the details of all four murders to date. He accordingly asked Cream to write down for him an account of his movements since first arriving in England. This Cream did, and it was immediately noticed that the writing was in the same hand as the letters at Scotland Yard. In addition they were written on writing-paper of American manufacture, unobtainable in Britain. Cream then taxed McIntyre with being suspicious of him, and of having him followed, and followed this with a similar letter of complaint addressed to the Chief Commissioner of the Metropolitan Police.

The police were highly intrigued by Cream's account of his movements in England, particularly by the gaps which coincided with the various murders. They questioned him further, and he told them he was the British representative of a firm of New York wholesale chemists, and showed them his sample bag which, they noted with interest, contained a quantity of strychnine hydrochloride pills and tablets. Cream explained that he took orders only from doctors and qualified pharmacists for these products.

In the meantime it had at last been decided to perform an autopsy on the remains of Matilda Clover. On 5th May the body was exhumed in Tooting Cemetery, and found to be in an excellent state of preservation, with deposits of strychnine still present. An inquest was arranged for 22nd June. The police, virtually certain that Matilda's last visitor had been Cream, did not arrest him immediately but issued him with a subpoena to attend the inquest. This he did, but was most unco-operative, refusing to give any evidence or even to admit to his correct name. The jury, however, after hearing the rest of the evidence, decided that Matilda Clover had died of strychnine poisoning, and that the strychnine had been administered by Dr Neill Cream. He was therefore arrested and charged with the murder of Clover, to which he made the odd reply, 'All right, but is anything going to be done about the other cases?'

Cream first appeared at Bow Street Magistrates Court in July, and was committed for trial at the Old Bailey. He was charged with the murder of Matilda Clover, Ellen Donworth, Alice Marsh and Emma Shrivell and for attempting to blackmail Dr Broadbent and Dr Harper. He was also charged with the attempted murder of another prostitute named Louise Harvey. This, it will be remembered, was the name of the girl coupled with that of Matilda Clover and mentioned in the letter Cream said had been shown to him by the non-existent C.I.D. detective, Murray. Though little had been heard of her she was to be an important witness at the trial later.

The police heaved a sigh of relief. At last they had caught the man who had been stalking the gas-lit streets of riverside London in a new and savage vendetta against the prostitute population.

The trial took place at the Central Criminal Court, before Mr Justice Hawkins, the same judge who had presided over the Lamson case ten years before. The trial lasted from the 17th to 21st October 1892, the prosecution being in the hands of the Attorney-General, Sir Charles Russell, Q.C. (later Lord Russell of Killowen). The prisoner was represented by Mr S. Geoghegan, Q.C., leading three juniors. Fifty-four witnesses were listed to testify for the prosecution, none for the defence.

Strange as it may seem, the charge against Cream for the murder of Matilda Clover did not seem all that secure if taken in isolation. It was largely a question of identity, and Cream, in pleading Not Guilty to all charges, strenuously denied that he had known any of the women involved and that the prosecution 'had got the wrong man'. If it rested on a matter of identity in one case only, a clever barrister like Geoghegan could easily confuse the jury and make them uncertain of their findings, and, as is well known, any uncertainty must be used in favour of the accused.

What the prosecution had to do, on that first day of the trial, was to obtain a ruling from the judge that evidence covering the other cases was admissable in the case of Clover. Such evidence showed a pattern of behaviour, the possession of strychnine and other incidents that would provide cumulative evidence of Cream's guilt. Both prosecution and defence were well aware of this situation, and Mr Geoghegan argued persuasively that only the evidence concerning Clover should be admitted. But Mr Justice Hawkes thought otherwise. He said that although the case rested largely on circumstantial evidence this was not unusual, for in most murders it was rare for witnesses to be present. His considered opinion was that all the evidence available showing Cream's previous behaviour should be admissable, and only by this means could the truth of the matter be ascertained.

With these arguments out of the way, the jury was sworn and the trial began.

The Attorney-General opened the proceedings by describing in outline the sequence of events from Cream's arrival in England in October 1891 until his arrest. He then began calling the first of the large number of witnesses for the prosecution, two of whom were the prostitutes Eliza Masters and Eliza May. They described how, after 'Fred' had made a date with them, he had instead gone off with Matilda Clover to her own lodgings and remained there until late.

Mrs Vowles, Clover's landlady, told of the girl's drinking habits, and how she thought she was having an attack of D.T.s. The maid, Lucy Rose, recounted how a doctor had been called who was of the same opinion as Mrs Vowles. In cross-examination it turned out that the 'doctor' who came was not a fully-qualified physician, but an assistant to the local general practitioner. He admitted that he had never experienced a case of strychnine poisoning, and that the idea of D.T.s had been suggested to him by Mrs Vowles. He had prescribed bicarbonate of soda and later the girl had been given potassium bromide by her regular doctor. The general practitioner said in his evidence that after he had seen the condition of his patient he expected her to die, and in view of her past history had had no hesitation in signing the death certificate as being due to alcoholic poisoning.

The evidence then moved on to the deaths of Marsh and Shrivell, and of the visit a few hours earlier of a man called 'Fred' answering Cream's description. Mrs Sleaper, Cream's landlady, said that the doctor had been inordinately interested in the account of the affair given in the newspapers, and shortly afterwards had astounded her by saying that he was certain the murders had been committed by his fellow lodger, young Harper.

Dr Harper gave further evidence of the letter he had received from 'M. Malone', later proved to be in Cream's handwriting, making the same accusation against his son. The police also gave evidence about the handwriting and about the American paper on which the note was written.

An important witness was a Mr John M'Culloch, who had met Cream in Canada on his return visit there during the first few weeks of 1892. He was a commercial traveller representing a coffee and spices firm, and had met Cream when both had been staying at Blanchard's Hotel in Quebec, at the end of February.

According to M'Culloch, Cream had indicated that he

was a medical representative for a New York firm of pharmaceutical manufacturers, and had shown him his sample-case. This included a bottle of white powder which Cream claimed was strychnine. M'Culloch's reaction to this had been, 'For God's sake, what on earth do you do with that?' to which Cream replied, 'I give that to women to get them out of the family way.' He also produced a pair of false whiskers and a beard, which he said he used 'to prevent identification when operating'.

Cream went on to tell M'Culloch that he lived in Lambeth and boasted of having had three women in one night for one shilling each. He talked constantly of sex, said M'Culloch, and at various times showed him pornographic photographs and pictures. He had not enjoyed Cream's company, but in the confines of the hotel lounge had had difficulty in avoiding him.

One by one the various witnesses gave evidence from the box, each adding a little more to the evidence against Cream. A surprising turn came when the prostitute Lou Harvey was sworn in. Her evidence was to put the eventual verdict beyond doubt.

In October 1891 Harvey had been picked up by Cream at the Alhambra Music-Hall and, after a few drinks, had spent the night with him at a hotel in Berwick Street. Cream had noticed that the girl had a few spots on her body and told her he was a doctor. If she would meet him again the following night he would bring her some pills that would alleviate the condition.

An appointment was made to meet the following evening near Charing Cross Station. Cream and Harvey met as arranged, and went for a drink in a pub in Northumberland Avenue, where Cream bought a bunch of roses for the girl. Afterwards they walked down to the Embankment. The plan had been to go to a music-hall again, but now Cream told Harvey that he could not accompany her there as he had an important appointment at St Thomas's Hospital at 9.30. Cream then gave her five shillings for the music-hall, and said he would meet her outside at 11.p.m., after which they would go once again to the Berwick Street Hotel.

Before leaving for the hospital, Cream gave her two gelatine capsules for her spots, and insisted that she swallow them there and then in front of him. For some reason which was never disclosed, Harvey was reluctant to do this. It is possible that she had begun to be suspicious of this mysterious doctor, who bore some resemblance to the description circulating of the man who had previously poisoned the other girls. At all events, instead of swallowing the capsules she threw them over her shoulder into the river. Cream looked at her hands to make sure she had taken the capsules and, apparently satisfied, walked off in the direction of Westminster Bridge. Harvey then hailed a hansom cab, went to the music-hall and waited for Cream after the show. By 11.30 he had not arrived, and the girl went home.

She saw Cream in the West End on two occasions afterwards, but he did not appear to recognize her.

At his trial, according to his counsel, Cream had never heard of Lou Harvey, but there was an interesting fact which undoubtedly connected him with the girl. Harvey had been living in a house in St John's Wood, No. 44 Townshend Road. She had been there only a week, and was not sure of the number. When Cream asked her where she lived, she made a mistake and replied, '55 Townshend Road, St John's Wood'.

A later witness, John Haynes, was to say that Cream had pointed out to him a house in Townshend Road where, he said, a prostitute found dead on the Embankment had lived. The house he pointed to was No. 55. At a later date Lou Harvey had seen reports in the press in which Cream had spoken of the letter in which her name was mentioned. She had immediately communicated with the police and

111

expressed her willingness to give evidence at the trial.

Mr Geoghegan's speech for the defence started with the admission that he did not really know where to begin. He had no defence witnesses, and could not put his client in the witness-box at that date even had he wished to do so. Most of his case, predictably, turned on the question of identifying Cream as the companion of the murdered women and the would-be-murderer of Lou Harvey. He made full use of the question of being 'reasonably certain' in the minds of the jury, and ended his speech as follows:

The Law of England . . . demands that the guilt of the accused shall be brought home to him as clear and as bright as the light of heaven now streaming into this Court; and it is under the protection of that figure that I leave my client, Thomas Neill Cream.

As was the custom of the time, the prosecution had the right of the final speech to the jury, and the Attorney-General did not take long to go over the incriminating facts once again. Then came the judge's summing-up, and the jury retired. They took exactly ten minutes to bring in a verdict of guilty.

The death sentence was then pronounced, but even while he was being led away Cream said to his warders, 'They won't hang me.' His forecast was incorrect. He was hanged at Newgate on 15th November 1892, and despite rumours that he had confessed his crimes to a warder, there is no evidence that this was so. He remained grim and silent to the end. Talkative as he had been in life, Thomas Neill Cream was not the confessing type.

Indeed, just what sort of man Cream was baffled many people at the time and has continued to be of interest to psychiatrists ever since. It is fairly certain that he caused the death of eight people — seven women and one man — during his medical career and, as he was a highly intelligent individual, he may have succeeded in covering his tracks in many other murders. Yet at the same time he did some extremely stupid things, such as drawing attention to the presence of strychnine in Stott's body in America and his extraordinary behaviour in writing a series of incriminating letters in England. We see here, perhaps, a form of conceit amounting to a death-wish in drawing the attention of the police to his actions.

Despite the letters that Cream wrote he was not, apparently, seriously attempting blackmail (though he had done so in America and Canada) for in no instance did he take any steps to collect the money. That he was a professional abortionist is certain, also that he had excessively strong sexual urges coupled with a degree of sadism. He suffered from sleeplessness and headaches, and, like Lamson before him, had recourse to morphine which, as a Victorian writer put it, 'saps the moral fibre and makes the victim unable to resist his morbid impulses.'

He did not come from a broken home, yet he exhibited criminal tendencies very early in his career. The very fact that his home-life was secure and that he was given more money and generally indulged more than his less-gifted brothers and sisters may well have had something to do with it. A secure home and an over-indulgent upbringing can produce a criminal as easily as a broken home and abject poverty — a fact that sometimes seems to be overlooked by today's psychiatrists.

6

Pierre Bougrat

(1887-1962)

During the summer of 1918 the French hospital ship *Patrie*
docked at the great naval base of Toulon near Marseilles.
Amongst the several hundred war-wounded it disembarked
was a handsome young captain from the Medical Corps who
had been severely wounded in the leg and had sustained
injuries to his head. When twenty-seven-year-old Pierre
Bougrat from Annecy had joined up in 1914, he had been a
medical student in the fifth and final year of his studies.

Bougrat was a brilliant student, and his war career had
also been noteworthy. At the holocaust of Verdun he had
been awarded the Croix de Guerre, promoted to captain in
the field, and later, in Yugoslavia, mentioned three times in
despatches. One of these citations had been for saving the
life of his closest friend, Jacques Rumèbe, with whom he had
fought side by side at Verdun.

The war-wounded from the *Patrie* were dispersed to
various hospitals and Bougrat found himself occupying a
bed in a converted school in the centre of Marseilles. He had
not written to his family, for he was a little sensitive about
his appearance and did not want to alarm them unduly. His
head injury forced him to wear his hair cropped like a
convict, he was thin and ill-looking and his leg was in
plaster. Perhaps understandably he had no desire to let his
family see him in this condition.

It was therefore with a certain amount of annoyance,
though coupled with pleasure, that a few days after admission into hospital he received two visitors. One was his

younger sister Juliette, the other his childhood sweetheart Lucie Arnaud. By the time Pierre had joined the army in 1914 it had been assumed by both the Bougrat and Arnaud families that the couple would eventually marry. But as far as Lucie was concerned, during the four years he had been away Pierre had been by no means a model correspondent. His few letters had been short, and had not been couched in very loving terms. To his own family he had hinted that, having seen the carnage of Verdun, with over a million soldiers killed or wounded, he had little inclination to marry and beget children who would become cannon-fodder for some future war engineered by the politicians.

The meeting of Lucie and Pierre at the bedside on that auspicious day was something of an embarrassment. Lucie detected a change from the fun-loving boy she had known before the war to the somewhat cynical and almost churlish man she now saw lying in the hospital bed. However, she had not forgotten their former 'understanding' and was determined to marry Pierre. Tactfully, Juliette Bougrat withdrew to do some shopping, leaving Lucie and Pierre together. She immediately reminded him of what their families were expecting, and asked Pierre if he was still of the same mind. The young man said he was prepared to honour the agreement, but put up certain objections. He was not yet qualified, for example, and could not support a wife until he had taken his final exams. Lucie's answer was that her dowry would be enough to see them through this period. And after that? Everything had been considered, enthused Lucie. Her father, who was Professor of Medicine at the Marseilles Medical School, would ensure that he got a practice. In fact, in the very same street in which the Arnaud family lived, a luxury flat and consulting-room had been recently vacated by a retired doctor, and Professor Arnaud was willing to purchase the flat and the practice and present it to his son-in-law as soon as he had qualified. Against this sort of argument there was little Bougrat could do. When Juliette returned from her shopping it was to learn that Pierre and Lucie were engaged and would be married as soon as he came out of hospital.

The wedding — a very grand affair — took place in Marseilles on 19th February 1919, immediately after Pierre's discharge from the army, and the couple took up residence in the luxury flat at 37 rue Senac provided by the father of the bride.

In March 1920 Pierre Bougrat completed his final year of study and qualified as a doctor. Late that year their daughter Gisele was born. Though the practice flourished from the start with the help of Professor Arnaud, it was not the sort of practice Bougrat really wanted. It was too 'fashionable', the majority of his patients being the wives of other doctors, lawyers, dentists, well-to-do local government officials and the like, most of them suffering from nothing worse than acute boredom. They flocked to his consulting-room with their imagined ailments, and one or two were not averse to hinting that they would appreciate a visit at home during the afternoon, when their husbands were otherwise engaged. Bougrat detested them all. He was much more interested in attending to the poor, usually free of charge, and openly boasted that he overcharged the rich deliberately in order to subsidise the needy. One of his patients was his old friend, Jacques Rumèbe, who lived in Marseilles and who had obtained a situation as wages-clerk in a large local factory. He had contracted syphilis during the war and came to Bougrat every Saturday morning for injections of the newly-discovered anti-syphilitic drug mercuric cyanide. As Bougrat was careful to explain to his friend, a cure was not guaranteed, but at least it would stop the infection from spreading.

Lucie Bougrat, brought up in the best Marseilles society and with plenty of money, was rapidly becoming more and more of a snob. She could not understand how her husband could spend time treating a man like Rumèbe, or, even remain friendly with him, when their social class was so different. Rumèbe had never achieved a higher rank than corporal throughout the war. It was useless for Bougrat to explain that in the carnage of battle, with friends falling at one's side, considerations of rank and social class became irrelevant. All Lucie knew was that the war had been over some time, and the most important thing in her life was the incessant dinner-parties she gave at the house.

Her husband never enjoyed these dinner-parties. He was not only bored but also concerned at the cost of these affairs, for Lucie was spending money at an alarming rate and seemed to think that her husband's practice provided limitless revenue. In fact many of the young doctor's patients suffered from that infirmity so often found in upper-class society — an allergy to the sight of a bill or at the thought of settling an account. Small wonder that Bougrat became more and more disillusioned with his wife's friends and their posturing. He began to absent himself from the dinner-parties earlier and earlier, usually retiring to his study to read. His conduct on these occasions did not please Lucie, and endless family rows were the result, often ending in Lucie's threat to leave her husband and 'go back to mother'.

For the sake of their daughter Gisele they remained together. Not did the couple enjoy a normal sex life, for Lucie thought the whole thing slightly vulgar and in any case did not want to run the risk of having more children. In this respect it was perhaps, the only thing the couple agreed on.

The incident which precipitated the break-up of the marriage occurred early in 1924. Thoroughly bored at one of his wife's interminable dinner-parties, Bougrat decided to go for a walk. His way led him, almost unconsciously, to a run-down quarter of Marseilles known as Les Allées de Meilhan, an area noted for its pimps and prostitutes. Walking down one of the ill-lit roads and scarcely aware of where he was, the doctor was accosted by a prostitute — something he did not particularly want just then. He was about to pass on when something made him look twice at the girl.

She was certainly very different from most of her kind. Tall and slim, with raven-black hair and enormous eyes, she was not only young and pretty but had a delightful figure. In addition she had the kind of outgoing personality that struck a responsive chord in the young doctor. Within minutes they were talking terms and the girl, who said her name was Andrea Audibert, conducted Bougrat to a sleazy boarding-house in the next street. There they were welcomed by the proprietor, Mme Honorine, a fat and greasy old woman who evidently knew Andrea well and silently gave her the key to a bedroom.

Later, in the room, Bougrat discovered that Andrea had once worked in an office, but having a sick mother and insufficient funds to obtain medicine, she had taken to the streets to augment her income. She worked, she said, entirely on her own.

Bougrat was totally enslaved by the girl. Sexually they were completely compatible and mutually exciting, and though Andrea had had experience of many men she was to say later that Bougrat satisfied her more than any other man she had ever known. The doctor was in his seventh heaven. Night after night he went to Mme Honorine's hotel to sleep with Andrea, returning to the rue Senac in the early hours of the morning hollow-cheeked and red-eyed. His behaviour became so erratic that even his friends began to shun him, and his practice shrank to nothing. Tales of his nightly excursions to Les Allées de Meilhan became common knowledge in the area, and salacious stories circulated about the love-sick doctor. Finally his wife could stand it no longer. Collecting most of her own belongings and taking Gisele with her, Lucie went back to her parents and began divorce proceedings.

Bougrat, meanwhile, though captivated by Andrea, was not so enchanted with Mme Honorine and her squalid surroundings. Several times he offered to install Andrea in a smarter flat in a better district, but each time she refused 'because of Mme Honorine'. Bougrat could not understand the hold the disreputable old lady had over Andrea, but was determined to find out. One night, when she again refused to tell him, he knocked her across the room. Tearfully she admitted her secret. She did not work alone, but under the control of her 'protector', a dockside apache called Paulo Fabiani. She was expected to have several clients in the course of an evening and if she upset the landlady, Mme Honorine would undoubtedly divulge all to Paulo. It was only Bougrat's generosity to her that had kept her mouth shut so far.

Bougrat's solution to this was a remarkable one. He himself would become Andrea's protector and he would 'buy' her from Paulo. Could the girl arrange a meeting with the apache? With noticeable reluctance she said she would try.

A few nights later Bougrat might have been seen entering the door of a dingy dockside café called The Tamarisk. Before long a vicious-looking individual followed him in and introduced himself as Paulo. After buying drinks the two men fell to discussing the price, Paulo demanding the sum of 30,000 francs for the girl, while Bougrat was not willing to give more than 8,000 francs.

At one point a fight broke out between the two men, and the café proprietor was amazed to see the gentle-looking and well-dressed doctor pinning Paulo down by the throat with one hand and raining blows on his face with the other. The fight ended as quickly as it had started, and once again the ill-assorted pair sat down and haggled over the price of the prostitute. A compromise was eventually reached by which Bougrat was to pay Paulo the sum of 4,000 francs immediately, and a further 400 francs a month for the next twelve months. In return, Paulo would release her to Bougrat that very day. Bougrat paid over the 4,000 francs and the deal was done.

Having come to a reasonably satisfactory arrangement with the apache, Bougrat moved Andrea out of Mme Honorine's questionable establishment and installed her for a few weeks in an expensive apartment in the rue de Rome. But the loss of his practice, and therefore most of his income, meant that the doctor was having a critical time financially. An expected legacy from his deceased mother was delayed by a technicality, and it was with undisguised relief that early in 1925 Bougrat saw his wife and child vacate the flat in the rue Senac for good. He brought Andrea to live there and gave up the lease of the rue de Rome apartment. But it was almost too late. His finances were such that he was already defaulting on the payments to Paulo. What friends Bougrat had once had on his own social level turned from him in disgust, most of them taking Lucie's side in the affair.

At first Andrea was pleased at being invited to live with Bougrat in his own home, and hopefully considered this a prelude to their getting married. But it soon dawned on her that things were not going at all well for the doctor. Where were the furs, the jewellery, the car, that Bougrat had promised her? Gradually disillusion set in, and Bougrat began to have as many quarrels with his mistress as he had had with his wife.

One day early in March Andrea happened to meet Paulo in the street. The apache suspected that things were going badly in view of the fact that his instalments were not being paid regularly. He tried to persuade Andrea to come back to him. He was much too scared to approach Bougrat direct, remembering only too well the thrashing he had received from the little doctor in The Tamarisk.

Andrea was not, at first, too keen. She distrusted Paulo, and determined that she would never work for him under the same conditions as before. Paulo hastened to reassure her that this time it would be different. He would obtain a smart flat in the St Cimiez district of Nice, where she would be available only by appointment. In that very smart district, with rich customers selected by him, and with the aid of the society veneer Andrea had acquired from Bougrat, he could guarantee her an income of 300 francs a month. Four or five days later she decided. She would go back to Paulo. While Bougrat was out one day Andrea packed her bags (not forgetting to include several valuable pieces of jewellery belonging to Bougrat) and took the train to Nice.

Bougrat was furious. Andrea's treachery made him bitter, and he was particularly angered by the thefts. Before the day was out he had lodged a complaint with the police accusing Andrea of robbing him, though he had no idea where she had gone. Now he was alone and apparently unwanted. From the window of his flat he could just see little Gisele playing on the balcony of her own flat just up the road. It was noticeable that whenever he looked her way she was made to come in from the balcony. Lucie Bougrat evidently had no intention of letting Gisele be contaminated by the sight of her immoral and lecherous father.

Bougrat was at rock-bottom, or so he thought. But there was worse to come. It stemmed from the astonishing sequence of events that began on Saturday, 14th March 1925.

Saturday was the day that Jacques Rumèbe regularly came to Bougrat for his anti-syphilis injections. Today was no different, and by the time Rumèbe rang the doctor's doorbell just before nine o'clock in the morning the syringeful of mercuric cyanide had been prepared and was waiting in the consulting-room.

Rumèbe was in a hurry, as he usually was on Saturday mornings. As wages-clerk at a local pottery it was his duty, every Saturday morning, to go to the bank and collect the firm's wages, which were distributed at noon at the factory. He normally went to the bank immediately after having his injection, and left the bank with the wages in a brief-case at about 9.15, getting back to the pottery fifteen minutes later. This sequence of events was well-known to Mme Rumèbe, though she was not aware of the exact significance of her husband's injections. He had told her they were in connection with a slight skin-rash.

On this particular Saturday, however, Rumèbe had his usual injection at nine o'clock, left the rue Senac soon afterwards but did not reach the bank until eleven o'clock. He gave no explanation of his lateness, but collected the money, leaving the bank about ten minutes past eleven, and was never seen again. When he had not returned to the pottery by noon enquiries were started and the disappearance reported to the police.

Despite his limited finances, Bougrat still managed to employ a couple, Henri and Augustine Prevost, to come in daily and see to his needs. At approximately 11 a.m. on the morning of Saturday 14th March Bougrat came into the kitchen, where they were polishing the silver. He told them he would be out for the rest of the day. He also told the couple not to bother to answer the telephone, and instructed them that under no circumstances whatever were they to go into the dispensary, which was situated behind the consulting-room. The Prevosts thought it all a little odd, but then their employer had been acting strangely for some time. In the event there were no telephone calls that day, but as the time went on the couple began discussing the reason why they were not allowed into the dispensary. They thought that perhaps the doctor had been conducting an experiment in the room and did not wish the equipment disturbed by the opening of the door.

Eventually their curiosity overcame them, and Henri

Prevost decided to have a look through the keyhole. What he saw mystified him completely, for within the narrow limits of the aperture he was just able to see what looked like the feet and lower limbs of a man apparently lying on the couch. On the floor was a brief-case which Prevost identified as belonging to Jacques Rumèbe. Mme Prevost then had a look and was as mystified as her husband. If the figure really was Rumèbe, neither of the Prevosts had seen him return to the flat since his departure earlier that morning. And again, if it *was* Rumèbe in the dispensary, why had Bougrat gone out, evidently intending to leave his friend there for the rest of the day? At six o'clock the Prevosts went home, leaving unsolved the mystery of the figure on the couch.

Bougrat finally returned to the flat just after midnight. His first action was to bring up a short ladder from the cellar into the dispensary. High up against one wall, immediately under the ceiling, was an unusual cupboard about six feet long and two feet high. Its double doors had been papered with the same design as the remainder of the room, and a stranger looking round the dispensary would have had no idea that the cupboard was there. Bougrat propped the ladder against the wall and opened the doors of the cupboard. He then went to the couch and picked up the body of his friend (for the corpse was indeed that of Jacques Rumèbe), and with the utmost difficulty managed to haul it up the ladder and place it in the cupboard. He closed the double doors, and completed his task by fetching a roll of wallpaper of the same design as had been used before, and papering over the doors. He was exhausted, but pleased with himself. At some later date, he thought, he would dispose of the body in a more permanent manner, but this would do for now.

It was only a day or two later that Bougrat received a visit from Jacques Rumèbe's wife. She was accompanied by a doctor named Louis Garrot who was the proprietor of a V.D. clinic Rumèbe had once attended. Garrot had remained a friend of the Rumèbe family, but had no time for Bougrat in view of his general behaviour and his treatment of his wife. Mme Rumèbe told Bougrat of her husband's disappearance, and asked if Jacques had said anything special, or acted in a peculiar way, the last time he had visited the doctor. Bougrat told her that he had noticed nothing unusual. Mme Rumèbe said that she was always nervous when her husband had to carry large sums of money about with him, and she was convinced that he had been attacked on the way back from the bank, robbed, and left for dead. What was worse, she continued, was that the factory-manager considered this theory to be over-dramatic and believed that Rumèbe himself had stolen the money and was lying low until the excitement died down.

Bougrat could give Mme Rumèbe little comfort, and could provide no theories about what Rumèbe had been doing between leaving the rue Senac just after nine o'clock and his arrival at the bank at eleven. Mme Rumèbe and Dr Garrot (who had been completely ignored by Bougrat during the interview) left, noting that the doctor seemed more and more nervous and ill at ease as the conversation continued. Bougrat decided that the sooner he moved the corpse out of the dispensary the better; but another incident put a stop to the plan.

Towards the end of March Bougrat had a second unexpected visitor. This time it was Andrea, worn and ill-looking and obviously at the end of her tether. Bougrat was so surprised at seeing the girl that he forgot to ask her in and had to be reminded of that fact. Once inside, Andrea told him that she had made a mistake in leaving him and wanted to come back. She had even brought back with her all the jewellery she had stolen, so Bougrat could now stop the police enquiries he had started.

What she did not tell Bougrat was that she had gone back to Paulo, only to discover that the 'luxury flat' in St. Cimiez was in fact a dockside brothel in the Vieux Port of Nice. She had escaped one night, and had come back to Bougrat as the only haven she knew.

The doctor, though still very much in love with Andrea, must have wished her timing had been a little better. There was the disposal of the corpse in the dispensary to be dealt with, but in the meantime he told Andrea that she could stay. When she asked him about his finances Bougrat said they were much improved, and went so far as to promise her a motoring holiday in Italy in a few weeks' time. The girl was delighted, and a few days later presented herself at the Mairie to obtain the necessary documents for the passports. One of these she filled in under her own name, giving her permanent address as 37 rue Senac. Her happiness was complete, and once again the girl began to have visions of marrying the doctor.

Her return to the flat was not greeted with much enthusiasm by the Prevosts. In the past they had had occasion to resent her 'lady-of-the-manor' behaviour and her tendency to order them about. Before long Andrea was once again complaining of how the flat was run, and in particular of a sickly odour that seemed to come from somewhere in the region of the consulting-room. Bougrat's theory, supported by the Prevosts, was that a dead rat was somehow lodged under the flooring; yet he would not agree to call in the Sanitary Department until forced to do so when the occupants of the next-door flat also began to complain. The Sanitary operatives duly arrived and sprayed a strong solution of formaldehyde everywhere, but if anything the smell became worse. Where did it come from? Henri Prevost suddenly remembered the strange cupboard high up in the dispensary wall. Could it possibly be coming from there? When he mentioned this to Andrea she snubbed him with

125

the remark that she did not know of the existence of the cupboard, and even if it did exist, how would a rat manage to climb into it? Prevost did not mention the matter again.

Towards the end of May two police inspectors presented themselves at 37 rue Senac and informed Bougrat that he was under arrest. They declined to provide a reason, but said the matter would be explained by M. Laures, the examining magistrate, the next day. At this examination the doctor was questioned about some cheques he had written during the past weeks. There was one for 2,000 francs in payment of a radio set. A cheque for 1,500 francs had been issued by Bougrat to pay his tailor's account, and within the last week there had been the issue of a cheque for 3,000 francs representing the deposit on a new car. All three cheques had been returned by the bank marked 'insufficient funds'.

In some ways Bougrat was relieved. Not a word had been said about Rumèbe or his disappearance, though the matter of uttering worthless cheques was a serious enough charge. He explained to the magistrate that when he wrote the cheques he was daily expecting to hear that the sum left to him in his mother's will had been deposited in the bank, and that there was therefore no intention to defraud. He was quite certain that if his creditors would allow him another three weeks' grace he would be in a position to honour all the cheques. M. Laures was not impressed and returned the doctor to gaol to await trial on a charge of false pretences.

Back in Annecy, Bougrat's father, a retired schoolmaster, got to hear of his son's predicament. Though they were not on speaking terms and had not been for some time, he felt the family honour must be retrieved. Accordingly, drawing all his savings from the bank, he came to Marseilles and sought out Laures. He offered to pay the disputed cheques immediately, on the understanding that all criminal proceedings against his son would be stopped. Laures agreed, but the legal machinery that had to be unravelled to achieve this took time, and Bougrat was forced to spend a few more days in prison. Those few days had fatal consequences for the doctor.

The mysterious disappearance of Jacques Rumèbe and the 25,000 francs was in the hands of one of the Marseilles police force's most experienced detectives. Chief Inspector Louis Robert was short and swarthy — a typical product of the great city in which he was born and where he had spent most of his life. On discovering that Bougrat was being held in prison pending the settlement of his debts he hurried to a magistrate to obtain a search-warrant for the flat in the rue Senac. At first the magistrate was hesitant and asked the Inspector whether he had reason to believe that Bougrat was connected with the disappearance. Robert told him that he had no direct evidence, but that Bougrat's flat was one of the last places at which the missing man had been seen that Saturday morning. He thought it advisable to have a look round and would feel happier if he had the authority to do so. The magistrate accordingly issued a warrant and Robert, in the company of his assistant, Inspector Dedieu, presented himself at the apartment. The door was opened by Andrea, who seemed frightened and nervous when she realized the two men were from the police. Robert and Dedieu were immediately struck by the foul smell coming from the flat. 'A dead rat,' said Andrea, 'that even the Sanitary Department has been unable to find.'

In Bougrat's consulting-room Robert pulled open a drawer in a desk and found the two new passports. He slipped them into his pocket and, somewhat to Dedieu's surprise, decided to call off the search and return to the Sûreté. There he showed the documents to the magistrate he had seen before and told him that, in his opinion, Bougrat and the girl were preparing to flee abroad as soon as Bougrat was released. 'To escape his creditors?' asked the magistrate.

'That, or to escape something worse,' replied the Inspector.

Robert then requested permission to continue his search of the flat, but this time with the doctor present. Robert knew that Bougrat had an astute young lawyer called Stephani-Martin who would be certain to lodge an official complaint if the flat were searched and Bougrat given no opportunity to be present.

The next morning Robert, Dedieu and two or three policemen returned with Bougrat to the rue Senac. The smell was as potent as ever, and seemed to come from the area of the dispensary. Bougrat was ill at ease while the search went on, and Andrea and the Prevosts were banished to the kitchen. Once the search-party was able to give its un-divided attention to the dispensary the presence of the curious cupboard high up in the wall was soon revealed. A ladder was fetched, and as one of the policemen mounted it he was stopped by Bougrat. Turning to the Chief Inspector the doctor said, 'M. Robert – in that cupboard you will find the body of a friend of mine who committed suicide in this room.' Robert asked him if that friend was Jacques Rumèbe, and Bougrat inclined his head.

'Open the cupboard, officer,' said Robert. The policeman did so, and recoiled with horror at the stench. Within the cupboard he could see a putrified form totally covered with maggots, which also infested the walls and ceiling. The form could scarcely be recognized as the human being it once was. Robert immediately sent for an ambulance, and the body was removed, an exercise that even the hardened ambulance-men were to remember for many years afterwards.

Bougrat meanwhile had been taken into the dispensary, and there Robert put the question directly to him – why had he murdered Jacques Rumèbe? By now Bougrat seemed to have recovered himself, and was almost cocksure in his answer: 'I did not murder Rumèbe. As I have just told you, he committed suicide in this room.'

128

The execution of William Palmer, 1856

Cartoons of George Bate, William Palmer and the 'Boots'

Thomas Smethurst

Buck Ruxton

Edward Pritchard

left Mary Jane Pritchard
right Mrs Jane Taylor, Edward Pritchard's mother-in-law

The trial of George Lamson at the Central Criminal Court
(the Old Bailey), 1889

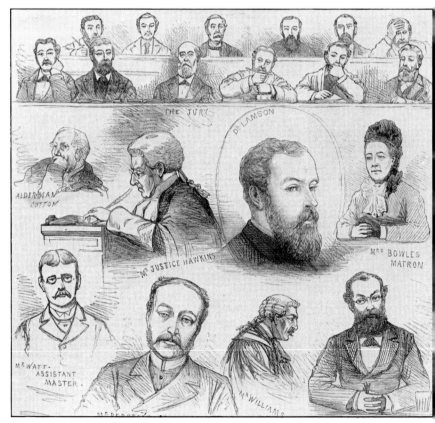

THE JURY

Dr LAMSON

ALDERMAN COTTON

Mr JUSTICE HAWKINS

Mrs BOWLES MATRON

Mr WATT ASSISTANT MASTER

Mr WILLIAMS

Some of the participants in the trial of George Lamson

left A highly dramatised representation of the discovery of the body
of Jacques Rumèbe in Dr Bougrat's surgery in Marseilles
right Police photograph of Pierre Bougrat immediately after his arrest

Pierre Bougrat in the dock

Marcel Petiot being interrogated after his arrest

left Petiot in the dock during his trial at the Seine Assize Court, Paris
right Police Commissioner Massu inspecting the incinerator where
the bodies were burned

Robert Clements with his fourth wife, Amy, after their wedding in 1940

Sam Sheppard wearing an orthopaedic collar for the injury he claimed he sustained when struggling with the mysterious bush-haired stranger

November 1966: Sam Sheppard is pictured leading his wife Ariane
from the courts after hearing he has been declared innocent
of the murder of his first wife twelve years earlier

Robert then invited Bougrat to explain just how this had come about. The doctor replied that Rumèbe had come to him for his usual injection that Saturday morning and had left for the bank just after nine o'clock. Bougrat had thought no more about the matter until just after lunch, when Rumèbe had come into the flat by the back entrance, obviously in a very agitated state. He was minus jacket and waistcoat and looked as if he had been beaten up. He told Bougrat that just after leaving him that morning he had met a former girl-friend and, despite the fact that he was on the way to the bank, had stopped to have a drink with her. He finally got to the bank about eleven o'clock, collected the money, and then went back to the girl's house for more drinks. Soon afterwards two men had come in, beaten him up and taken the money from his brief-case and then thrown him out into the street. He had come to Bougrat for help and to see if the doctor could lend him 25,000 francs to replace the stolen money.

Bougrat had had to explain that he was unable to help but that he might be able to obtain most of the sum from a friend who lived nearby. Leaving Rumèbe alone in the consulting-room he had gone to this friend, only to find that he was not in. When he returned to the rue Senac at about 4 p.m. he found Rumèbe lying on the floor in a semi-conscious condition. Before he died he was just able to tell the doctor that he had poisoned himself with mercuric cyanide.

Chief Inspector Robert listened to this tale with scepticism. Why had Bougrat not informed the police when he found his friend had killed himself? 'Well,' said Bougrat, 'as the money was missing from the brief-case there was a strong chance the police would think I had stolen it. I therefore decided to try and find this girl-friend of Rumèbe's and see if I could get the money back, but unfortunately I could not find her.'

Bougrat then described how he had put the body in the

cupboard late at night after the Prevosts had gone home. Asked if Andrea had been a party to the affair, Bougrat pointed out that on 14th March Andrea had already left him. Her return at the end of that month had, in fact, been something of an embarrassment to him as it interfered with his arrangements for disposing of the body.

At this point Robert decided to arrest both Bougrat and Andrea. The pair were taken before a magistrate, Bougrat to be charged with the murder of Jacques Rumèbe, Andrea as an accomplice.

The discovery of Jacques Rumèbe's body and the arrest of Bougrat created a sensation in the Marseilles area. The local newspaper, *Le Petit Marseillais*, carried grossly inaccurate reports of the discovery and supposed murder while at the Sûreté Robert was bombarded with anonymous letters accusing Bougrat of having murdered practically every patient who had died while under his care. Though most of these stories were palpably nonsense, some, Robert decided, warranted further examination.

One such was a letter, in an obviously feminine hand and signed 'A Friend of Justice', accusing Bougrat of having murdered a woman patient living in the rue Consolat. She had been a patient of Bougrat's for two months, said the writer, when she died on 5th April that year. Bougrat, while attending her, had robbed her of jewellery worth 20,000 francs which she kept in a tin-box under the bed.

With the assistance of the Registrar of Deaths and Burials the inspector was able to identify the dead woman as Thérèse Dumonchois, aged forty-three, a former music-hall artiste who had lived at that address with a man-friend. When Robert went to see the man at the rue Consolat, he confirmed that Thérèse had indeed been a patient of Bougrat's for two months prior to her death. But there was no mystery about it. She had died of tuberculosis after a long illness, and as for the jewels, they were still in the tin-box and not one

130

was missing. With the man's help Robert was able to trace the writer of the letter, an old colleague of the dead woman, who, when confronted by Robert with the truth, merely maintained that even if Bougrat had not stolen the jewellery she had a 'feeling' that he must have murdered Thérèse Dumonchois. The woman was fortunate that Robert did not charge her with obstructing the police in their duties.

Another story concerned a man named Dominique, the proprietor of the Bodega bar on the famous Canebière. On the day before Rumèbe's disappearance, the story went, Bougrat and Dominique had been gambling at cards in the café and the doctor was losing heavily. Just before the game ended Dominique collapsed and was taken up to his flat above the café while Bougrat, instead of attending to his friend, vanished with all the proceeds of the game. Though a doctor was called, Dominique died later that day. Robert dutifully investigated this story, only to find that nobody could confirm Bougrat's presence in the café that day (though he was known to gamble heavily with Dominique) and that the doctor who attended Dominique had certified death as due to peritonitis.

Stories of this kind circulated widely in the area from the time of Bougrat's arrest until his eventual trial.

As a prisoner on remand in the enormous Chave Penitentiary at Marseilles, Bougrat was allowed a certain amount of freedom and the concession of being allowed to talk to other prisoners in a similar situation. One man with whom he became friendly was Gauthier du Roy, a confidence trickster of some repute. Part of his act was to pose as an ex-Army officer of high rank, for which purpose he wore the ribbon of the Croix de Guerre and that of the Légion d'honneur. As a seasoned resident of quite a few state penitentiaries, du Roy numbered many friends amongst the inmates, and told Bougrat that, for 'a consideration', one such friend could be of value to him. This was a man called Dervin, at present in prison on a manslaughter charge. For a payment of 25,000 francs to du Roy, Dervin would confess that he was the one who had attacked Rumèbe and robbed him on 14th March.

Bougrat distrusted du Roy though, like many others, he could not help liking him. Quite apart from distrusting him, Bougrat was in no position to pay a sum of this magnitude, and told du Roy so. Du Roy was annoyed, and perhaps to get his own back on Bougrat, but certainly to ingratiate himself with the authorities, told the prison governor that in conversation with Bougrat the doctor had confessed to the killing. According to du Roy, Bougrat had described how Rumèbe had returned to him later on that fateful Saturday, with his brief-case full of money, and how Bougrat had given him another injection of mercuric cyanide, sufficient to render him unconscious. He had then forced him to inhale fumes of prussic acid, which had killed him.

In accordance with the usual procedure in France, Bougrat was questioned further about this by an examining magistrate, but denied ever making such a confession.

The legal system in France is such that a very long time may elapse between the arrest of a criminal on a serious charge such as murder, and his eventual appearance in court. Once arrested, a suspect is brought before a *juge d' instruction* (examining magistrate) who, over a lengthy period, collects all the evidence concerning the accused presented by the police and examines it thoroughly. He keeps in constant touch with the detectives as their investigations continue, and interviews and examines witnesses for the prosecution and for the defence. Only when he considers that all the known facts are available does he decide whether or not a prima-facie case has been made out by the police. This, of course, may take a considerable time and accounts for the lengthy period between arrest and trial. The French themselves are well aware of this problem, and, though often criticized, maintain that a man or woman on a serious charge will have a fairer trial when press and public interest has waned and the facts can be presented unemotionally and viewed in proper perspective. There is, of course, the risk that an accused person may spend a year or more in prison and then be acquitted by the jury, as may happen in Britain when a man is remanded in custody. The alternative — a quick trial while public interest is still high and emotions aroused — can lead to the situation that marred the trial of Dr Sam Sheppard in Ohio in 1954, and no doubt Civil Rights propagandists in various countries will long continue to debate the subject.

It was not until 23rd March 1927 that the doctor finally stood trial at Aix-en-Provence, the legal headquarters of the *département* of Bouches-du-Rhône.

The trial president was the noted judge Bringuier, assisted by two 'assessors', while the case for the prosecution was in the hands of the elderly and ascetic-looking *maître* Siame. Defending Bougrat was his old friend, and former guest at many of the rue Senac soirées, Jean-Michel Stephani-Martin.

Bougrat was accused of the following crimes:

1. That on 14th March 1925 he wilfully and with premeditation caused the death of one Jacques Rumèbe.
2. That at the same time he robbed Rumèbe of a sum of money amounting to 25,000 francs.

Before the trial opened the President warned the jury that in the course of the proceedings they would probably hear much to Bougrat's discredit about his morals and private life, but that they must remember they were not trying him for this, but for murder and theft only. This was a salutary warning, for as so often happens in France and America the Press had pre-judged the issue and was already referring to 'the murderer Bougrat' long before the trial began.

The prosecution produced a formidable number of witnesses, beginning with the Prevosts, who described how they had looked through the keyhole on 14th March and seen the feet of a man in the dispensary, and what they were quite sure was Rumèbe's brief-case lying on the floor. Mme Rumèbe made a brief but hysterical appearance, but more impressive was the evidence of her friend Dr Garrot, who had come with her to Bougrat's flat and who spoke tellingly of Bougrat's intense nervousness during the ensuing conversation. Garrot also made the point that in his opinion Rumèbe was no longer suffering from syphilis, and there was therefore no reason to give him any injections of mercuric cyanide.

Undoubtedly the witness who created the most sensation was Andrea herself. Soon after Bougrat's arrest it had been decided that she could have no possible connection with the murder of Rumèbe and she had been released. Here, at Aix-en-Provence, she described her first meeting with Bougrat, his repeated promises to buy her costly gifts and her gradual disillusionment when she realized that he had very little money. Her original 'protector', Paulo Fabiani, she mentioned little, and indeed, he had vanished very early in the proceedings and could not be found. In the newspaper accounts of the trial Andrea's appearance is commented on, the general consensus of opinion being that this *femme fatale* was not really beautiful but had 'very fine eyes'. Not for the first time was it queried how a man of Bougrat's taste and judgement could have come under the spell of such an ordinary person.

Gauthier du Roy, by then serving a term of imprisonment for false pretences and unlawfully wearing military decorations, was an important prosecution witness with his tale of Bougrat's supposed confession in prison. But when his record was revealed it did not take Stephani-Martin long to discredit him as a witness, and his evidence was not taken too seriously by the jury or the President of the Assize. At the same time there *was* the evidence that the dose of mercuric cyanide found in the body was not a fatal one, and Rumèbe therefore *could* have been killed in the way du Roy described, as the presence of prussic acid would have been very difficult to detect, particularly if it had been inhaled.

An important defence witness, and almost the only one, was Professor Barral, a distinguished toxicologist, who stated that after he had completed a full post-mortem of the remains he could find nothing to indicate that Rumèbe had died by poisoning. He was also of the opinion that, had Rumèbe been unconscious, it would have been impossible for Bougrat to have forced him to inhale fumes of prussic acid.

Bougrat's own defence was presented to the jury by Stephani-Martin. He contended that Jacques Rumèbe had certainly come to Bougrat for his usual injection at about nine o'clock on the Saturday morning, but later, at about eleven, he had returned after going to the bank and had requested another injection as he considered the first not strong enough. Bougrat was a little unsure about doing this but, wishing to satisfy his old friend, he had given him a second injection of mercuric cyanide of the same strength as the first. The total strength of the two injections was far below that calculated to be a fatal dose and it was with the utmost horror, said Stephani-Martin, that Bougrat had seen his friend collapse and die before his eyes within minutes of receiving the second injection. He could account for it only by assuming that Rumèbe was over-sensitive to the action of the drug. Bougrat had panicked, hidden the body, and kept the money. The later arrival of Andrea had made it virtually impossible for him to get rid of the corpse, and when questioned by the police he had invented the story of Rumèbe's attack and his subsequent suicide. He was the first to admit that he had been a fool and also admitted the theft of the money. But quite definitely, said Stephani-Martin, his client

135

was not a murderer. Particularly could he not have been the murderer of his wartime friend, Jacques Rumèbe, remembering that he had been decorated on the field of battle for saving the life of that very same man.

The trial had taken twelve days and had been the main talking point throughout France. At the end the jury were asked to ask themselves the following four questions:

1. Did Pierre Bougrat kill Jacques Rumèbe?
2. If so, was the murder premeditated?
3. Did Bougrat steal the money from Rumèbe?
4. If so, were the two crimes connected?

The jury took only thirty minutes to give an answer in the affirmative to all four questions. Bougrat, invited by the President to say a final word in mitigation, preferred to remain silent. Amid scenes of intense excitement and emotion the President then sentenced the doctor to hard labour for life on the penal settlement of Devil's Island. An appeal was entered by Stephani-Martin but rejected by the Supreme Court in September 1927. Two months later Bougrat joined three hundred other prisoners on the convict-ship *La Martinière* and set sail for South America. He was never to see France again.

The French convict settlement of Devil's Island was in reality a group of three islands situated five miles off the coast of French Guiana. It consisted of the large island from which the colony took its name, together with the two smaller islands of St Joseph and Isle Royale. Part of the settlement included the mainland port and trading-post of Kourou, and it was here that the more educated and intelligent convicts were imprisoned.

The colony had been established by the French in 1852. For most of its hundred years' existence conditions were appalling and mortality extremely high. Notorious for its brutality and killings, as well as deaths from yellow fever and leprosy, it was popularly known amongst French convicts as 'The Dry Guillotine'. It was finally closed by the French in 1948, when it had a population of over three thousand, though the last convict did not officially leave until 1952. Many had nowhere to go, and to this day the families of convicts, and even some convicts themselves, are to be found living in the region.

It was at this dreadful and forbidding place that Bougrat and his fellow-convicts landed just before Christmas 1927. As a doctor Bougrat was welcomed by the prison governor and immediately set to work in the large hospital on the mainland. It soon became apparent that the chances of escape were small. The doctor was told of various attempted escapes that had come to nothing, including the deliberate murder of four convicts so that their bodies could be lashed together to form a raft.

Having come through so much, and with a bleak future before him, Bougrat felt he had little to lose. Together with three or four friends he evolved an escape plan and began gathering together stocks of anti-malarial and other drugs for the journey. In his special position as hospital doctor he was trusted more than most and had more contact with the outside world. By June 1928 his scheme had been perfected. He and his friends were secretly to make a boat out of a tree-trunk. Provided with medication and food the party was to leave Kourou one evening at dusk and paddle along the coast, travelling only at night, to the mouth of the river Moroni which formed the boundary between French and Dutch Guiana. Having achieved this, the plan was to journey up the river and its tributaries, passing through cannibal-infested jungle, to reach their eventual goal, the frontier with Venezuela.

Bizarre as the plan was, and fraught with danger, it succeeded. Bougrat and his friends left Kourou undetected, and twenty-three days later, after incredible hardships and adventures, arrived at the frontier town of Ipara, in Venezuela. Here, thinking they were safe, the party gave itself up, only to find that a price had been put on their heads by the French. They were immediately arrested and arrangements made to ship them back to Kourou.

It so happened, however, that the wife of the mayor of Ipara had just given birth to a child and was dying of puerperal fever. With what remained of his stock of drugs, and with his expert knowledge, Bougrat was able to save the woman's life. So delighted was the mayor that he not only cancelled the order for their return but gave them every assistance, with guides and safe-conduct passes, to enable them to cross Venezuela and reach the capital, Caracas.

During his fight to save the life of the mayor's wife, Bougrat had been assisted by an Italian nurse called Maria Stocchia. She had been brought to South America as a child by her father, who had dreamed of making a fortune there, but unfortunately he had died and she had been left stranded. She, too, wanted to reach Caracas. By the end of September 1928, Bougrat and his companions, including Maria, had reached the capital. Here another disappointment awaited them, for they were advised that the French government was intending to request a repatriation order for them. But once again fate took a hand. A few days after their arrival in the capital the district was smitten by a violent earthquake. For his work amongst the victims, particularly in the outlying villages, Bougrat became something of a national hero.

Once the crisis was over he married Maria and settled down in Caracas as a general practitioner. By then he had become so famous that the Venezuelan President, General Gomez, refused to act on the repatriation order when it came, and Bougrat and his new wife were permitted to remain in Venezuela and were granted honorary citizenship.

Bougrat died peacefully in 1962 at the age of seventy-five, one of the best-loved physicians in the land that had given him shelter. In 1970, in the village in which he died, a marble memorial was erected bearing the legend, 'In memory of Pierre Bougrat, an exemplary citizen and doctor who earned the affection, admiration and respect of all who knew him.' It was the end of the long journey from the rue Senac.

7

Buck Ruxton

(1899-1936)

Most doctors are considered by their patients to be of rather more than average intelligence. Certainly they have qualified in their profession after several years of concentrated study and even if (as some claim) the passing of examinations is not always a test of intelligence, at least it betokens a reasonably retentive memory and an ability to assimilate facts. Yet when a doctor turns to crime intelligent behaviour often flies out of the window, and, despite his qualifications, his actions and instincts descend to the level of his most ignorant and untutored patient. In so many cases, his mind ceases to be the tool of an intelligent man and his actions become dangerous to himself and often verge on the downright stupid. The extraordinary behaviour of Palmer and Pritchard, to name only two, adequately underlines this point. If, along with engineering the crime itself he is faced with the problem of disposal of the bodies, he may well find himself as unequal to the task as any illiterate.

Dr Buck Ruxton of Lancaster was a highly experienced practitioner and a good surgeon. As far as his work was concerned he was a thoughtful and efficient physician, but faced with a double murder and the necessity of getting rid of the bodies, he acted in such an extraordinary and suspicious manner that the case is almost without parallel in the annals of murder.

The story begins in the town of Lancaster where, in September 1935, Dr Ruxton was living with his wife and three small children in a substantial stone-faced house at 2

Dalton Square. The doctor was Indian, and had been born Bukhtyar Rustomjii Hajin in Bombay in 1899. When he came to England in 1925 and qualified as a doctor he found it convenient to change his name by deed poll to 'Buck Ruxton'.

His wife was called Isabella and hailed from Edinburgh where she had first worked as a waitress before marrying a Dutchman named Van Ess. In 1928 her marriage had been dissolved owing to her association with Ruxton, and she had been living with him since that year, first in Edinburgh, then in London and finally in Lancaster. Though never legally married, they had three children, the eldest seven years of age in 1935.

The doctor had purchased his substantial practice in 1930. Whilst Ruxton was extremely popular, his home life was somewhat tempestuous and the couple became notorious in the town for their frequent and violent quarrels. On more than one occasion the police had to be called to Dalton Square when Ruxton had offered violence to his wife.

The trouble was jealousy on the part of the doctor — jealousy of a kind that was instant and uncontrollable. He suspected his wife of infidelity on the slightest provocation, and any inadequately-explained absence on her part, even for a few hours, was seen by him as proof of dalliance with another man. Ruxton was later to say, 'We were the kind of people who could not live with each other — yet could not exist without each other.'

On Saturday, 14th September 1935 Isabella Ruxton borrowed her husband's car and went to Blackpool to see the lights. She left on her own, but in Blackpool she was due to meet her two sisters who had travelled down from Edinburgh for the same purpose. This was an excursion the sisters arranged together every year.

They apparently enjoyed themselves and saw 'all the fun of the fair', and Mrs Ruxton's departure from Blackpool was delayed until 11.30 p.m. She arrived back in Lancaster well after midnight, to be greeted by her husband, who was by then in a towering rage.

What exactly happened that night is open to conjecture, but what is certain is that it resulted in the death of two women. Mrs Ruxton was strangled in the course of a violent quarrel, and her cries for help caused the maid, twenty-year-old Mary Rogerson, to come to the assistance of her mistress. As the only witness of the murder she, too, had to be disposed of, and was probably bludgeoned to death. Ruxton then undressed the bodies, carried them up to the bathroom and spent the rest of the night draining them of blood and then dismembering and mutilating them.

As a doctor he was naturally well-versed in anatomy, and the job was done efficiently. The mutilations were intended to remove identifying features, but in this the doctor excelled himself. The very removal of such features was later to draw the attention of the police to what the murderer was trying to hide, and so contributed to the identification of the corpses. But that was a long way ahead.

Having worked all night, Ruxton then took the various pieces into the adjoining bedroom where he wrapped them in torn sheets, some pillowcases and a blouse and rompers, all identified later as having belonged to the women or coming from the house.

Cleaning up afterwards was a long and gory process, and Ruxton had not completed it by 6 a.m. on the Sunday morning. At that point he realized that Mrs Oxley, the charwoman, was due at seven o'clock, and immediately went round to her house to tell her not to come that day. The reason he gave was that his wife and Mary Rogerson had gone on a trip together to Edinburgh and would not be back for a few days. He then returned home, gave the children their breakfast (unaccountably they do not seem to have been disturbed by the events during the night) and later that morning took them to a dental colleague in Morecambe, whom he asked to look after them for a few days as his wife was on holiday. The dentist, well aware of the constant rows between Ruxton and his wife, assumed that this was a euphemism to hide the fact that another family quarrel had taken place, and gladly agreed to have the children.

Though he had told Mrs Oxley not to come that morning, on arriving back in Lancaster Ruxton immediately called on a patient who also did housework, Mrs Hampshire, and asked if she and her husband could come round that afternoon and help with the cleaning.

When the Hampshires arrived they found a scene of utter chaos. The walls and the stairs had been stripped of paper, plaster removed from the bathroom walls, the stair-carpet taken up and straw seemed to be everywhere. There were pools of water all over the floor and Ruxton told the astonished Hampshires that he was getting the house ready for the decorators who were coming while his wife was away; this time the story was that Isabella and Mary Rogerson had gone to Blackpool.

Less easy to explain were the yellowish-brown stains in the bath, which came to within a few inches of the top, and the discovery of small pools of blood here and there in the house. Ruxton explained the blood by saying that he had cut his hand while opening a tin of fruit. Mr and Mrs Hampshire thought the whole thing very odd, but at that stage had no suspicions of foul play. They got on with restoring some semblance of order to the premises, though neither was successful in removing the stain from the bath despite several applications of Vim. When they had done what they could, Ruxton thanked them and gave Mrs Hampshire a blood-stained suit which he said might 'serve a turn' for her husband, and some equally badly-stained carpets. The carpets, when later soaked in water, produced a reddish-coloured fluid.

Early on the morning of Monday 16th September Ruxton went to Mrs Hampshire and asked if he could have the suit back. She said it was already at the cleaners — though this was not so. The doctor's appearance was dishevelled, he was unshaven with no collar and tie, and was wearing an old raincoat. He looked, she said, extremely ill. Later that morning the regular char, Mrs Oxley, went to the house for the second time (there had been nobody about at her usual time of seven o'clock) and was let in by Ruxton. She described him in similar terms.

Later that day Ruxton took his car in for servicing and borrowed an Austin as a replacement. The following day, on the Carlisle to Glasgow road near Kendal, he was stopped by the police for not having reported a collision with a cyclist. At the police station he appeared very agitated and said he had been to Carlisle on business. After depositions had been taken he was allowed to go home.

During the next 36 hours there was much activity in the doctor's house. A bonfire was started in the yard and Mrs Oxley and two other women who were employed by the Ruxtons from time to time noticed that in the flames were several items of clothing recognizable as belonging to either Mrs Ruxton or Mary Rogerson. There was also the odd fact that the doors of two upstairs rooms were locked.

On Thursday 19th September Ruxton rose early, brought his own car to the back entrance of Dalton Square and, for the next hour or so, was observed by neighbours going back and forth to the house apparently loading a large number of parcels. He finally left the house at eight o'clock and returned at 3.30 p.m. telling Mrs Oxley he had been to Blackburn.

During the day Mrs Oxley and the two other women had been about their duties, and noticed that the upstairs rooms were now unlocked. From the rooms came a nauseating smell, and on Ruxton's return they complained about this.

144

The doctor's answer was to send one of them out for a large bottle of eau-de-Cologne which he sprinkled liberally everywhere.

Understandably, there had been several enquiries from friends as to how Isabella and Mary were enjoying their holiday. The Rogersons were particularly surprised that their daughter had gone off without telling them, for though she lived in she saw her parents almost every day. Ruxton began giving different accounts to different people — stories that revealed odd inconsistencies. To one friend he said that the women were touring Scotland in his own car, but the next day he was seen driving it in Lancaster. To another enquiry he supplied the information that his wife was in Blackpool.

To the Rogersons he told the most surprising story of all: that Mary had been secretly associating with a local lad and was pregnant. Mrs Ruxton, he said, had taken her away 'to try and get the trouble over.' Mr and Mrs Rogerson found this difficult to believe. They had no knowledge of any boy-friend or any impending marriage, which Mary would surely have told them about. When given the news by Ruxton, Mr Rogerson said that he did not care what Mary's condition was, he wanted her back by Saturday or he would report her as missing to the police. Ruxton assured him that he would get his daughter back and asked him not to go to the police.

After this incident the doctor's attitude to his wife's disappearance underwent a complete change. Until then he had expressed no concern regarding her departure. But a week later he began to put it about that his wife had left him. He told a Mr Jefferson that he thought his wife had run away with a young man from Lancaster called Edmondson, and that he had been suspicious of their friendship for some time. He also went as far as saying that he believed his wife had been promiscuous with many men, visiting them in

145

various places, and that Mary had connived at this and often went with his wife on these clandestine trips.

By now the children were back with him at Dalton Square and he wrote to Isabella's sister in Edinburgh:

I am heartbroken and half mad — Isabella has again left me. She has done this trick again after about ten months. Do you remember she left me bag and baggage last November? The children are asking for her daily and I really cannot sleep without her . . . Mine is only temper, but in my heart she is all.

He also mentioned young Edmondson to the police and said that on a previous occasion the young man and Mrs Ruxton had gone to Edinburgh and stayed at the Adelphi Hotel under false names. He went to the police on various occasions, apparently concerned at his wife's disappearance. On one such visit he told them that the telephone-operators had informed him that they had overheard 'silly love-talk' between his wife and Edmondson at the Town Hall, where the latter worked. The police began to get more and more suspicious of Ruxton, particularly after the grisly discoveries in Scotland at the end of the month.

On 29th September a Miss Susan Johnson was staying at a hotel in Moffat, a village just off the A74 main road between Carlisle and Glasgow, some 20 miles from Dumfries. During the morning she went for a walk and had occasion to cross the bridge which carried the road over the little river Linn, at Gardenholme. Looking down into the gully she saw what appeared to be a human arm protruding from some wrapping. She quickly returned to the hotel and told her brother, and when he arrived at the bridge he was able to see various parts of a human body wrapped in newspapers and a torn sheet. Mr Johnson immediately notified the police, and later that afternoon a full search was mounted by officers from Dumfries. The immediate result of this search led to the discovery of four bundles of human remains.

The first contained two upper arms and four pieces of flesh, and was wrapped in a blouse. The second bundle, wrapped in a pillowcase, contained two lower-leg bones, two thigh-bones, two upper-arm bones and several pieces of flesh. The third parcel contained seventeen pieces of flesh and was wrapped in a torn sheet, while the fourth bundle, also wrapped in a sheet, held the chest portion of a human trunk and two legs and feet.

In addition to these four bundles other remains were scattered about over a wide area. They consisted of two human heads, a thigh-bone, two arms with hands attached and various pieces of flesh and skin. During the next few days more remains were discovered higher up on the banks of the river Linn, and in the river Annan which joins it. These included a pelvis, some portions of flesh, an arm with the hand attached and another thigh-bone. In all, with the other fragments discovered in the vicinity by blood-hounds, over sixty pieces of human remains were found scattered over a wide area, though the majority were centred on the confluence of the Annan and the Linn. They appeared to consist of the remains of two human bodies, though their condition at first made it difficult for the police to ascertain the sex of the victims. From the appearance of the pelvis, one was undoubtedly a woman, but for some time after the discovery the police were under the impression the other body was that of a man. Both appeared to be well-developed and well-nourished and both had been extensively mutilated, with eyes, ears, nose and lips removed, and the teeth extracted after death. The finger-tips had also been removed, presumably to avoid identification. It was noted too that the bodies had been dissected cleanly and neatly with a surgical knife, obviously by a person with medical knowledge and skilled in anatomy.

The daunting task of re-assembling the bodies and trying to gain some idea of how they looked in life was entrusted to a team of Scottish forensic experts headed by Professor John Glaister, Regius Professor of Forensic Medicine at the University of Glasgow, and Professor J.C. Brash, Professor of Anatomy at the University of Edinburgh. At a later stage they were joined by Professor Sidney Smith, Regius Professor of Forensic Medicine at the University of Edinburgh.

In the meantime the police had their own investigations to carry out. The remains had been wrapped in various materials including some newspapers, the *Sunday Graphic* and the *Sunday Chronicle* of 15th September (the day the women had disappeared) and the *Daily Herald* of a few days earlier. It was the *Sunday Graphic* that proved to be of particular interest, as this was a special 'slip' edition carrying details of the recent carnival at Morecambe , and printed for distribution only in the Lancaster and Morecambe area a hundred miles away from Moffat. This immediately alerted the police to the possibility that the bodies came from that area, and details of missing persons were sought. With the co-operation of the Lancaster police it was soon found that the Rogersons had recently reported the disappearance of their daughter, and it was noted that her employer, Mrs Isabella Ruxton, was also missing from home.

Ruxton, meanwhile, had once again written to Mrs Nelson, his sister-in-law, saying that he wanted to meet his other sister-in-law, Mrs Trench, to find out what had happened to his wife. Ruxton went to Edinburgh and met the sisters at a family conference. Mrs Trench, having read of the discovery of the bodies at Moffat, suggested they might be those of the missing women and asked Ruxton if he had 'done anything' to Isabella. Ruxton became extremely excited and replied, 'I would not harm a hair of her head. I love her too much. I do not stand to make a penny by her death.'

He then returned to Lancaster, and the next day went to the police in a highly agitated state. He said that newspaper reports linking the bodies with the two missing women were all 'damned nonsense' and that the rumours circulating in the town were ruining his practice. He was told by the police that they had no control over what appeared in the press. At the same time they took the opportunity of asking him if he had ever given away pieces of stained carpet. He said he had, as they were worn out.

By this time Ruxton was becoming seriously worried at the direction of the enquiries the police were making. During the next few days he approached several acquaintances apparently with the idea of persuading them that they had seen Isabella and Mary during that fateful week-end. To one man, a plumber, he suggested that he had come to mend the lavatory cistern on the Sunday night, and had seen Mary then. The man denied it, for the very good reason that he had been in bed with 'flu all that week-end and had done no work at all. Ruxton also went to Mrs Hampshire in great agitation and asked her if she still had the suit he had given her. When she said she had, he implored her to get rid of it and to 'stand by him' if any enquiries were made about it.

On 11th October Ruxton began to compile a lengthy document entitled 'My Movements'. The only reason one can give for this action is that Ruxton was increasingly worried about the police, and wanted to have a clear statement to give them when the time came. On the same day he insisted on seeing Captain Vann, the Chief Constable of Lancaster, and in an interview in which he became steadily more agitated and incoherent, he implored Captain Vann to issue a statement saying there was no connection between the Moffat bodies and his missing wife and maid. Vann, to calm him down, said he would do so as soon as he was satisfied that this was really the case.

On the following day, 12th October, he was invited by Vann to attend Lancaster Police Station. There he found the Chief Constable together with several members of the Scottish C.I.D. He gave the 'My Movements' document to Captain Vann, and was afterwards asked to make a statement, which he read over and subsequently signed. After a further consultation between Vann and the Scottish police, Ruxton was arrested and charged with the double murder of Isabella Ruxton and Mary Rogerson. He replied, 'Most emphatically not. Of course not. What motive and why? What are you talking about?'

The following day he was formally charged at Lancaster Magistrates Court with the murder of Mary Rogerson. He was then remanded further every week, as the law requires, and on 5th November was charged with the additional murder of Isabella Ruxton. On 13th December he was committed for trial at Manchester Assizes.

The trial of Dr Ruxton began on 2nd March 1936 and lasted eleven days. The affair had generated intense interest world-wide, and reporters from newspapers of several countries thronged the press-benches. The judge was Mr Justice Singleton, and Mr J. C. Jackson, K.C., Mr Maxwell Fyffe, K.C. and Mr Hartley Shawcross appeared for the Crown. Ruxton was defended by Mr Norman Birkett, K.C. leading Mr Philip Kershaw, and instructed by Mr Edward Slinger, solicitor, of Lancaster. There were no less than 107 prosecution witnesses but no defence witnesses except Ruxton himself.

The strength of the prosecution case depended very largely on the identification of the bodies. The fact that two females from Ruxton's household had vanished mysteriously, and two female bodies had been discovered a hundred miles away in Scotland, was not conclusive evidence. Halsbury's *Laws of England* (Section 9, Article 768) is explicit on this point:

Where no body or part of a body has been found, which is proved to be that of the person alleged to have been killed, the accused person should not be convicted either of murder or manslaughter unless there is evidence either of the killing or of the death of the person alleged to have been killed. In the absence of such evidence there is no onus upon the prisoner to account for the disappearance or non-production of the person alleged to be killed.

From the above it is obvious that Ruxton could not be convicted unless it could be proved conclusively and beyond reasonable doubt that the Moffat bodies were those of Isabella Ruxton and Mary Rogerson. For this reason the medical evidence was of paramount importance and was the main feature on which the case turned. It will therefore be dealt with in some detail.

The actual reconstruction of the bodies had been undertaken by Professor Brash in an anatomical *tour de force* that had no precedent in medico-legal history. The starting point had been the decision that because two heads had been found, the remains must represent two human bodies. These were later classified as Body No. 1 (Mary Rogerson) and Body No. 2 (Isabella Ruxton). From that point it was necessary to work downwards and assign all the various pieces to one or other of the bodies. Seventeen separate limb portions were so assigned, the problem being made slightly easier in some respects by the fact that Body No. 2 was older and more heavily-built than the other. On the other hand this initially confused the issue, as the absence of a pelvis for Body No. 2 allowed the pathologists to conclude that it was a male. A painstaking putting-together by Brash of the several limbs of each body proved this conjecture to be wrong, as the contours and limb proportions of Body No. 2 established its femininity.

The ages of the bodies were determined by X-ray examination of the bones and by the appearance of the skulls. From these findings, and from the evidence of a dental expert, Dr Hutchinson, it was decided that Body No. 1 was probably between eighteen and twenty-two years of age.

151

Mary Rogerson was just twenty. Body No. 2 was obviously older, and the estimated age was thirty-five. Isabella Ruxton was thirty-four.

From the formulae used by the comparison of the longer bones, the approximate height of each body had been calculated, and these in turn coincided to within half an inch with the heights of Mary and Isabella.

The most dramatic part of the medical evidence lay in the description of the mutilations carried out on the victims after death. When these mutilations were compared with what was known of the physical characteristics of the missing women, a systematic pattern was revealed. It was obvious that an attempt had been made to remove all identifying features.

Mary Rogerson, for example, had a slight cast in one eye. The eyes of Body No. 1 had been removed. Instead of the usual three vaccination marks on the upper arm, Mary had four, together with a birthmark nearby. All the skin in that region had been removed.

Mrs Ruxton had medium-brown hair, but though the head of Body No. 2 had been scalped, enough hair remained to reveal its original colour. She also had a somewhat large nose; the nose of Body No. 2 had been removed. She wore a denture and had rather prominent teeth — most of the teeth of the body had been extracted after death. She had suffered from a condition which caused her lower limbs to swell, making them the same thickness from knee to ankle. The legs of Body No. 2 had had the soft tissue of the legs cut away, though this had not been done with Body No. 1. Finally, Mrs Ruxton's toes were deformed and she had a large bunion. The one available foot of Body No. 2 had had the toes removed, and bore what appeared to be the marks of an excised bunion.

Professor Brash produced in court a plaster model of one foot of each corpse, dressed in silk stockings, and demonstrated that one fitted exactly into the shoes of Mary and the other into those of Isabella. The professor's final achievement was the production of life-size photographs of the heads of the women when alive, and photographs of the skulls found. When superimposed these were found to coincide exactly, and a tiara worn by Mrs Ruxton was found to fit perfectly on the skull of Body No. 2.

This form of photographic reconstruction was thought to be unique in a criminal case of this kind, though defence counsel, Mr Norman Birkett, tried hard to persuade the judge that this evidence was too inaccurate to be admissable. He did not succeed and was over-ruled.

Professor Glaister, in his evidence, gave an account of the large number of blood-stains found at Dalton Square, both on the premises and in the drains, and proved that they were human blood. They were also too extensive to be the result of a simple cut with a tin-opener, as Ruxton claimed. Various articles of clothing, including the blouse and the rompers in which the remains were wrapped, were also produced, and identified by witnesses as coming from the Ruxton house. The torn sheet was an important item and was identified by an expert as part of a sheet found on the Ruxtons' bed, due to a fault in the warp that was common to both pieces. There was also, of course, the damning evidence of the *Sunday Graphic* special Lancaster edition used to wrap some of the remains, and it was proved that a copy of this edition had been delivered to Dalton Square on the Sunday morning of the murders.

The evidence for the prosecution had taken nine days, and it was not until Thursday, 12th March, that Mr Norman Birkett began his closing speech for the defence. He said he was astonished at the Crown's contention that it was necessary only to identify the Moffat remains as Mary Rogerson and Mrs Ruxton to convict the prisoner. Even if they were identified as such, and had, in fact, been murdered, there was still nothing to connect them with the prisoner, who at all times had said he had no idea where the missing women were, or what had happened to them.

He also made much of the fact that Mrs Oxley and Mrs Hampshire, though noting the state of the stairs and walls in the house and the bonfire in the yard, had no suspicions of crime at the time. He put it to the jury that the evidence they had eventually given in court had been suggested to them by the prosecution after other facts had been discovered.

According to Birkett, blood in and around a doctor's surgery and in the drains was a perfectly natural condition and he suggested that the blood-stains on the stairs could have been the result of a miscarriage sustained by Mrs Ruxton some time before, when she had collapsed in the hall and was carried upstairs to her room.

He ended by commenting on the extraordinary reconstruction carried out by Professors Glaister and Brash and their subsequent identification of the corpses. Nevertheless he reminded the jury once again that the finding of the murdered women at Moffat did nothing to prove they had been murdered by Ruxton a hundred miles away in Lancaster. In his opinion the Crown had failed to prove their case beyond reasonable doubt, and therefore a verdict of not guilty was the only course left open to them.

Mr Justice Singleton's masterly address to the jury took up most of Friday, 13th March, and the jury retired at 4 p.m. One hour and five minutes later they were back and returned a verdict of guilty. An appeal was lodged, but dismissed, and Dr Buck Ruxton was hanged at Strangeways Gaol, Manchester, on 12th May 1936. During his last hours he wrote a full confession of his crime, which was printed in a national newspaper, in which he described how he killed his wife in a fit of rage, and then had to kill Mary Rogerson, who was the sole witness.

The Ruxton children were taken into care and spent several years in a Children's Home at Croydon, Surrey, far removed from the scene of the affair. The house at Dalton Square has had no tenant since, and has been used mainly as a storage place by the cinema next door. The blood-stained bath is still in position.

Soon after Ruxton's execution children in Lancaster and district were singing the following ditty to the tune of 'Red Sails in the Sunset':

> Red stains on the carpet
> Red stains on the knife,
> Dr Buck Ruxton
> Has murdered his wife.
> The maid put her head in
> To see what's to do —
> Dr Buck Ruxton
> Then murdered her too!

It remains a grisly reminder of one of the most blood-thirsty medical murders of the twentieth century.

8

Marcel Petiot

(1897-1946)

The process of war results in the transformation of generally-accepted standards; actions which are reprehensible in peace-time become praiseworthy in conflicts between nations. During the last war, in France and in many other occupied countries, quiet men leading peaceful lives, going about their work and raising families, sometimes turned into ruthless killers when the object of their hatred was the German army and all it represented.

Admittedly, it must be said that some took advantage of this reversal of standards to remove enemies and business rivals on the pretext of their alleged collaboration with the Germans. But few embarked on such a well-organized plan of wholesale murder as did the French physician Dr Marcel Petiot in Paris during the period from 1942 to 1944.

Petiot himself admitted, with pride, to the murder of sixty-three men and women, all described by him as 'German soldiers and collaborators'. When, at his trial, it was pointed out that clothing found in the cellars of his house included many articles of children's wear, he blandly explained that some German soldiers were very small for their age!

Petiot's career as a murderer almost certainly began many years before the Second World War. He was born in 1897 in Auxerre, in the *département* of Yonne. By the time he was thirteen both parents were dead and he was brought up by an aunt who apparently displayed little enthusiasm for him. This was understandable, for by all accounts he was a particularly unpleasant child. Cruel and sadistic by nature, he took pleasure in maiming and torturing small animals, and on one occasion strangled the family cat in a fit of temper. That night he slept with the corpse cradled in his arms and wept profusely.

In 1915 he left school and became a registered medical student (perhaps it was felt that his investigations into animal anatomy fitted him particularly for this calling). His introduction to medicine lasted only a year, and in 1916 he was conscripted into the French army.

Petiot's army career was not without incident. He worked as a medical orderly in a field hospital but in 1917 was severely wounded by the premature explosion of a hand-grenade he was examining. This appears to have affected him psychologically and he was sent to the mental hospital at Orleans for observation. Petiot objected to this most strongly and after a few weeks was returned to his unit at his own request.

It is possible that his enforced absence from his unit resulted in the temporary cessation of his 'business' act-ivities, for only a short time after returning to the field hospital he was court-martialled for stealing drugs and sell-ing them to addicts − something of which he had been suspected for some time. Fortunately for him he had an excellent lawyer, who pleaded that the offence had been committed while Petiot was mentally unstable due to his injuries. The court gave him the benefit of the doubt and decided not to proceed with the matter on the understanding that he undertook psychiatric treatment in Rennes. Here he stayed for two years, finally being demobilized in 1919 and returning home to Auxerre, where he was treated as an out-patient at the local hospital.

Throughout his time in hospital he had continued his medical studies, and despite his supposed 'mental insta-bility' he not only succeeded in qualifying as a doctor in

1921, but also received 'honourable mention' for his thesis on hereditary paralysis. What is even more astonishing is that in 1923 he was finally examined by an Army medical board, certified as an epileptic, and awarded a 50 per cent pension!

In 1924 he moved from Auxerre to Villeneuve, a town in the same *département* and some seventy miles south-east of Paris, where he acquired a practice as a general practitioner. With his charming ways and dark good looks he was an immediate success, displaying no symptoms at all of the epilepsy with which he was said to be afflicted. He entered local politics as a staunch Socialist, and in 1925 was elected mayor of Villeneuve.

The strength of his popularity may be gauged from the fact that he managed to survive a scandal the year before his election. Petiot had as his housekeeper a young girl called Louise Bonnet, and it was no surprise to the residents of Villeneuve when she became pregnant by the doctor. The French, are, perhaps, more tolerant of sexual mis-demeanours than are other nationalities, and no doubt Petiot, as a doctor, could have 'arranged' things without too much publicity. Whether or not he attempted to abort the girl is not known. What *is* known is that shortly before she was due to give birth she vanished completely. The police investigated the matter thoroughly but could not account for her disappearance despite receiving an anonymous letter stating that Petiot had murdered the girl and disposed of her body. No trace of the luckless Louise was ever found and years later, when Petiot's past was being eagerly unearthed by journalists, it was found that all police records of the case had disappeared.

Even with this sinister story circulating about him, Petiot was not only elected mayor in 1925 but in that same year married Georgette Lablais, a pretty brunette and daughter of a wealthy father who ran a highly fashionable restaurant in Paris. Less than a year later their son, Gerard, was born.

A relatively quiet period followed, but in 1928 Petiot was charged with, and subsequently convicted of, bypassing the electricity meter at his surgery and so obtaining free light and power. He was given a suspended sentence, but as a convicted criminal his resignation as mayor was automatic. Such was his popularity in the town, however, that nobody could be found to stand in his stead, and he was re-elected. Later he was also elected as a *membre du conseil* for the *département*.

Although he was undoubtedly popular, Petiot never seems to have been able to keep out of trouble and the year after his re-election he was charged with stealing several cans of petrol from a garage. In this instance he was fortunate, and the investigation was dropped through lack of evidence. But more serious trouble was on the way.

In 1930 a Mme Debeuve, manageress of the local co-operative dairy, was found strangled and a considerable amount of money stolen from the premises. Strong rumours in the town connected Petiot with the crime, and for the first time his popularity began to dwindle. The police investigated, and were able to find a man who said he had seen Petiot hurrying from the scene of the crime just before the body was discovered. This alone was not enough to bring a charge, and Petiot continued attending to his practice as normal. The witness who had identified him happened to be one of his patients, a man he was treating for rheumatism. A few weeks later the patient died suddenly, and Petiot certified the death as being due to natural causes.

This time feeling in the town was totally against him and he was obliged (for the second time) to resign as mayor. He continued in practice, however, as there were still enough patients who had faith in him, but finally, in 1933, decided to leave Villeneuve permanently and seek his fortune in Paris.

In the capital he bought himself a practice at 66 rue Caumartin near the Place de l'Opera. The rue Caumartin, in the ninth *arrondissement,* was a busy and populous area. Shops, often with their owners living above, lined both sides of the street while here and there offices intruded, with the occasional block of flats.

Petiot's apartment was not easily distinguishable from the many others in the street, but being a born publicist he quickly remedied that.

DR MARCEL PETIOT

Diploma of the Faculty of Paris 1921,
Membre du Conseil for the département of Yonne,
former house-physician in hospitals and asylums —
and a Medical Officer of Health for the Department
of Seine.

The notice on his front door went on to describe the 'up-to-date and modern' equipment available to patients, and reminded them that because of 'the most rapid means of transport being always available' the doctor could reach his patients within minutes. In fact, this meant that he had a motor cycle.

Undoubtedly Petiot was a good doctor. To his patients he brought sympathy and understanding, displaying real compassion for the poor and those unable to meet his fees. On more than one occasion he treated a seriously-ill child of impoverished parents free of charge, and would willingly see a working man on a Sunday if that was the only day he could attend the surgery.

Perversely, and in spite of a fresh start, Petiot could not keep out of trouble. In 1936 he was arrested for stealing scientific books from a shop in the Boulevard St Michel. Examined by a police doctor, Petiot succeeded in convincing him that he was mentally unstable, and the charges were dropped on condition that he spend a month in a mental clinic at Ivry. What is curious is that these various bouts of so-called mental instability were never reported to the French Faculty of Medicine and there was never any question of his permit to practice being withdrawn. Even more curious is the vast amount of money Petiot seemed to have at his disposal. Not only did he buy both the practice and the property in ths rue Caumartin, but in 1940, soon after the occupation of Paris by the Germans, he bought a fifteen-room villa in the ru Le Sueur just off the avenue Foch near the Arch de Triomphe. This had formerly been the home of Cécile Sorel, the famous French actress, and cost him several million francs.

As well as paying cash for the property, Petiot arranged for extensive alterations to be made. A peculiar triangular room next to the double garage had its windows bricked up and a spy-hole inserted in the wall. Under the garage floor a pit was constructed and covered with boarding while the existing boiler was replaced with one which was much larger than the premises needed, even in winter. Round the garden of the villa the doctor had a high wall built, effectively isolating the projects.

Many people were inquisitive. To those who asked questions Petiot said that he was converting the premises into a small mental hospital as he wished to specialise in psychiatric treatment. Certainly he must have known far more about the subject than the average doctor.

Although the new premises in the rue Le Sueur were much more spacious than those in the rue Caumartin, Petiot did not move his family to the larger house. Indeed, he did not use any of the fifteen rooms in the house itself, but confined his activities to setting up a consulting-room in the garage. Sparsely furnished, with one desk and two chairs, it gave on to a short corridor which led to the peep-hole giving a view of the interior of the mysterious triangular room.

By the time Petiot had made all his alterations the Germans were well installed in Paris and a host of new regulations had come into being. Not all were imposed by the Germans. Marshal Pétain, the ailing and elderly hero of the 1914-18 war, was in command of Occupied France, and many decrees were issued by the puppet French government in his name. In view of the alarming depletion of manpower, coupled with the falling birth rate, one such decree was to impose the death penalty on anyone either performing or having an abortion.

The patients coming to the rue Le Sueur were very different from those attending the rue Caumartin. At the new premises there seemed to be an element of secrecy and it is fairly clear that Petiot intended to carry on there his former occupation of supplying drugs to addicts and also procuring abortions. In the Paris of 1941 people risked their lives daily in evading the curfew and the host of regulations in force. The fear of the guillotine certainly did not deter the many backstreet abortionists from continuing in business, nor doctors willing to oblige for a fat fee.

An early patient at the rue Le Sueur was a young married woman called Denise Hotin. She was a Parisienne, and early in 1941 had married Jean Hotin, the not-too-bright but wealthy son of a prosperous farmer in Neuville-Garnier, only a few miles from Paris but deep in the heart of the country. Denise knew little of country ways, and cared less, and as a result was not popular with her in-laws. Despite the shortage of man-power she refused to do her share of work on the farm. Notwithstanding the presence of the Germans in Paris, she constantly pined for her beloved city and was apt to make disparaging remarks about the dullness of life in the country.

A few weeks after her marriage, Denise discovered that she was pregnant. She and her husband, like many other young couples at the time, saw only a bleak future ahead and

162

had no wish to start a family under such inauspicious conditions. After some discussion with her husband (but not with his family) she decided to get an abortion. Obviously this could not be done at Neuville-Garnier, and arrangements were made for her to go to Paris.

In July of that year she and her husband travelled to the capital and stayed in a hotel near the Gare St Lazare; Denise went off on her own to see a midwife who was said to be able to arrange things. This midwife did not undertake abortions herself and sent Denise to see Dr Petiot in the rue Caumartin, just round the corner.

Petiot was not very keen at first, apparently, probably because Denise did not have enough money on her to pay the deposit. He told her to come back in a fortnight's time when, in any case, her 'condition' would be more conducive to treatment. Denise and her husband thereupon returned home, though for some reason Denise made no mention to him of the visit to Petiot but gave the impression that the whole matter remained in the hands of the midwife.

Two weeks later Denise once again made the journey to Paris, this time alone. She stayed with an old friend of her family, a Mme Mallard, and Petiot, it is almost certain, came to the house and performed the operation. Two days later Denise returned to Neuville and resumed her uneasy relationship with her husband's family, but in her absence tongues had begun to wag. Village gossip insisted that she had been to Paris to get an abortion, and though this was precisely what she had done, she became thoroughly frightened that the gossip might reach the ears of the police and her life be in danger as a result.

She suffered the village's innuendoes until the spring, but then decided to go to Paris again, seek out Petiot, and obtain from him a certificate showing that she had certainly had an operation, but for something other than an abortion. It was, perhaps, an over-optimistic idea, but she went to Paris in

May and once again stayed with Mme Mallard. The day after her arrival she told her friend she was off to see Dr Petiot, and from that moment she was never seen again.

Back at Neuville-Garnier life went on much as ever, and Jean Hotin does not seem to have been much concerned about his wife's absence. It is possible that they quarrelled immediately before her departure, and her lack of communication was accounted for in that way. At all events it was several months before he roused himself sufficiently to take any action.

That November he went to Paris and called on Mme Mallard. He was told by her daughter of his wife's intended visit to Dr Petiot. This was the first time that Jean Hotin had ever heard the name, and he went to the rue Caumartin only to find the doctor out on his rounds. He was due back at five o'clock, but as it was not yet four o'clock and Hotin had a train to catch, he decided not to linger and returned to Neuville-Garnier. He made no further effort to find out what happened to Denise and subsequently obtained a divorce on the grounds of desertion.

Petiot, meanwhile, had been finding more and more clients for his rue Le Sueur surgery. One was a pimp and a drug addict called van Bever who came to Petiot for supplies. Unfortunately the sole source of his income, a prostitute named Jeannette Gaul, was serving a term in the women's prison at Suresnes and he was unable to pay. Petiot refused to grant him credit or supply the drugs, and van Bever promptly threatened to report him to the police as a trafficker in heroin. The doctor then pretended to relent and told van Bever that he would supply him, but that he would have to return the next day as he had no 'hard stuff' on the premises.

It is known that van Bever called at the rue Le Sueur the following day. No one ever saw him again. Released from prison, Jeannette Gaul made enquiries and eventually contacted Petiot, who told her blithely that the missing man was in the hands of the Gestapo. On hearing those dreadful words, Jeannette made no further enquiries for fear of implicating herself. She assumed that van Bever had been transported to Germany, as had so many who fell into the hands of the German Secret Police.

It was about this time, early in 1942, that Petiot first had the idea of using would-be refugees as a source of steady income. Near him in the rue Caumartin lived a Polish Jew called Joachim Gruschinov who was in business as a furrier. It was obvious to Gruschinov that Jews in France, though at the moment still left in peace, would almost certainly soon become subject to the harrassment and persecution meted out to them in Germany. He spoke of his fears to Petiot, who was his doctor, and who had previously hinted that he was a member of the Resistance and could arrange to smuggle people out of the country in return for a fee. This fee, Petiot hastened to add, did not go to him or to the Resistance, but was needed to 'grease the palm' of various individuals on the escape route.

After some hesitation, Petiot said that he could probably arrange to have Gruschinov smuggled to South America, but it would cost him a great deal of money. Gruschinov was to give Petiot all his money and valuables, which would be sent on ahead, and come to the rue Le Sueur in secret late at night. The Pole naïvely agreed to this plan and told his wife of the scheme, promising to send for her when he arrived in South America. Tearfully she packed his bag, and carefully sewed into the lining of his suit a thousand dollars in small notes. Gruschinov had also been told to remove all identification from his clothes and belongings, as he would be travelling under a false name. This done, Gruschinov presented himself at the doctor's surgery.

The next day Petiot told Mme Gruschinov that her husband had begun his journey, and gave her the torn half of

165

a hundred-franc note. When he gave her the other half, said the doctor, it would be a sign that her husband had arrived in South America safely. Mme Gruschinov never received the second half of the note, and her husband was never seen alive again.

A similar incident took place in connection with a Dr Paul Braunberger, a Jewish general practitioner living near the rue Caumartin and therefore a business rival of Petiot. He, too, was convinced that the persecution of Jews would shortly begin in France, and asked Petiot's advice about an escape route. Petiot told him he could arrange an escape through Spain for a fee of 1,000,000 francs. Braunberger took some days to accumulate this amount, but finally collected it and took it in cash to the rue Le Sueur.

Braunberger had not told his wife of his sudden decision to make a bid for freedom, and she was greatly surprised when, on the very day he was visiting Petiot at his surgery, she received a letter from him explaining what his intentions were. He told her that it was certainly for the best, that he would make arrangements for her to join him, and that in the meantime she was to put all his most valuable possessions in a trunk and await further orders.

During the weeks that followed she received various letters purporting to come from her husband, but in a disguised writing due, he said, to the fear of identification. The letters enjoined her to the utmost secrecy, to tell friends and neighbours that he had been taken ill while visiting a private patient far from Paris, and finally to send the trunk and its contents to Petiot at the rue Le Sueur.

But Mme Braunberger was a little suspicious. In particular, she did not like this idea of sending all her husband's valuables to Petiot's surgery, for she had been hearing some odd rumours regarding large sums paid to Petiot and the complete disappearance of the people involved. In addition there was the handwriting and contents of the letters themselves. All the letters began 'Ma Chérie' – a form of address never used by the doctor, who always began his letters 'Chère Maguy'. Again, several phrases in the letters were quite alien to Braunberger and the way he normally wrote. Mme Braunberger decided to wait a little while and not forward the trunk. After a few more days of agonized thought she at length went to the police and officially reported her husband as missing. She told them of the letters and the instructions regarding the trunk, but though the police took careful notes they apparently took no further action at the time.

Other mysterious disappearances took place, all connected in some way with Petiot. An entire family of Jews, M. and Mme Kneller and their eight-year-old son, also vanished after paying the doctor 1,500,000 francs. Later a mysterious individual, subsequently identified as Petiot, collected their belongings on a handcart from a reluctant concierge.

Early in 1943 Petiot had engineered the 'escape' of certain well-known characters in the Paris underworld. They included those with such picturesque names as François the Corsican, Jo the Boxer and Chinese Paulette. When friends began to make enquiries about their ultimate destination, the trail always stopped at Petiot. Amongst these friends was Pierre Beretta, an escaped prisoner-of-war living precariously in Paris under a false identity. He decided he could not run any further risks, and when he asked about the possibility of escaping from France he was told about Petiot. Unfortunately the Gestapo caught Beretta before any arrangements could be made, and to save his skin he turned informer. The fact that Petiot could apparently organize escapes was revealed and the doctor immediately arrested.

It is not absolutely certain what Petiot told the Gestapo at first, for he was in something of a quandary. If he refused to say anything he would almost certainly be tortured and later shot. If, on the other hand, he confessed, the Gestapo might hand him over to the French civil authorities, which would be little better. Petiot played his cards carefully. He finally confessed to the Gestapo that he had committed murder many times, but stressed that his victims were all Jews and that he was, therefore, assisting the Third Reich of ridding Europe of 'this scum'.

It took over seven months for Berlin to investigate this story, but finally, just before Christmas 1943, he was released by the Germans and returned to his family. Whatever they thought of Petiot as a man, they no doubt found it useful that a Frenchman was doing their dreadful work for them, and with such success.

Petiot returned to his 'practice' with renewed vigour, for in his absence touts had been soliciting for him and unearthing prospective clients who had the neccessary cash. No doubt the doctor felt safe, believing that the Gestapo would protect him should the truth ever leak out.

For the real truth was that not a single Jew had been smuggled out of France by Petiot. All those who had visited the rue Le Sueur had been killed, most probably having been persuaded to have a final anti-typhoid injection. Looking through the peep-hole into the triangular room he had dispassionately witnessed their death agonies, later collecting their clothing and belongings and storing them neatly on racks in the garage. Needless to say, all cash had been taken from the victims, and this, together with the large fees demanded, meant that Petiot must have netted many millions of francs during the two years of his activities.

One of his greatest problems was the disposal of the bodies. He began by ordering large quantities of quicklime, delivered at night, but supplies became difficult and the builders' merchants concerned a little too inquisitive. He therefore began burning the bodies in the great furnace installed on the premises. This was to be his undoing.

The large number of clients awaiting him on his release from the hands of the Gestapo caused Petiot to act carelessly. Body after body was packed into the furnace and left to burn while the doctor went about his normal business. At length the inevitable happened. On the afternoon of 11th March 1944 the chimney caught fire while Petiot was absent.

At 22 rue Le Sueur, opposite the surgery, Mme Marcais had been getting more and more annoyed by the thick, dirty and evil-smelling smoke billowing round the premises and invading every room. When her husband returned home from work at six o'clock she persuaded him to cross the road to No. 21 and remonstrate with the doctor. This Marcais attempted to do but could get no reply to his loud ringing of the doorbell. By this time flames were shooting out of the chimney of No. 21 and, fearing the building would soon catch fire, Marcais telephoned the police.

The call was answered by officers Teyssier and Fillion. From the concierge of the house next door they obtained the information that No. 21 was owned by a Dr Petiot, whose actual home was at 66 rue Caumartin. They contacted the doctor by phone and, on hearing the news, he immediately asked if they had been able to get inside the house. Petiot seemed very relieved when they told him that they had not, and said he would be there in ten minutes. When he had not arrived in half an hour the two policemen decided to call the fire brigade.

When the fire brigade arrived the corporal in charge broke one of the windows, released the catch, and gained entry into the house. After looking round the ground floor, and guided by the stench, they found their way down to the basement. All round the furnace, on the floor, were dismembered arms, feet and legs. Another pile of severed limbs and incomplete torsos stood waiting in the corner. The stench and fumes were appalling, and the firemen had dif-

169

ficulty in not vomiting as they attempted to empty the furnace which was choked with material and control the fire.

The moment the fire brigade corporal recognized what he was dealing with he sent an urgent message to the police upstairs. Teyssier and Fillion went downstairs, and were equally nauseated by the sight. Staggering upstairs again to the comparative fresh air of the ground floor Teyssier went to telephone his headquarters.

While he was gone a smartly-dressed man arrived, asked to speak to the policeman in charge, and told Fillion that he was the brother of the owner of the property. Fillion took him to the basement and opened the door. The man (later identified as Petiot) took one look and shut the door hurriedly. The pair then went back upstairs, where Petiot drew Fillion aside. 'If you are a good Frenchman,' he said, 'do not be alarmed at what you have just seen.' He went on to say that he was the head of a Resistance Group, and that all the corpses downstairs represented the bodies of German soldiers and French collaborators. The whole affair must be kept quiet, he continued, for if the Gestapo got to hear of it, his life and those of all his Group would be in serious danger.

Teyssier, who had by then returned, listened to this explanation, but told Petiot he would still have to report the matter to his superiors. 'I understand that,' said the doctor, 'but for goodness' sake be discreet about it.' With that, Petiot departed, and Teyssier noted that he had come on a motor cycle.

Teyssier's second report to H.Q., revealing the presence of the bodies in the basement, precipitated immediate action. Members of the Paris *police justiciaire* (the equivalent of the British C.I.D.) began a thorough examination of the premises. The main part of the house revealed nothing but odd bits of furniture covered with dust-sheets, and was obviously not used. The outbuildings were a different matter. Apart from the corpses in the basement, the second garage was found to contain enormous quantities of clothing and personal possessions. Later they were to discover a bureau with a drawer containing lists of all Petiot's victims, with names, addresses and dates of 'escape'. Petiot was nothing if not methodical.

It is fairly evident that at this stage both the two policemen and their superiors believed the story that the victims were German soldiers and collaborators executed by the Resistance. It was not until the next day, when they studied the lists more thoroughly, that they realized that most of those listed appeared to have Jewish or German-Jewish names. The presence of children's clothing also seemed to require an explanation.

Believing Petiot's story, the police took good care not to publicize the matter on that first day and it was not until the evening of the following day that they decided to visit the doctor at the rue Caumartin. It was also on that day that the press, alerted by rumours running rife in the *quartier*, learned that something serious was afoot and descended in hordes on the rue Le Sueur. The secret of the belching chimneys and the mutilated corpses in the furnace-room became instant headline news, read avidly by a public both fascinated and repelled by the story.

When the police finally went to the rue Caumartin they found the place deserted and the Petiot family missing. A café proprietor opposite was to say that on the evening of the 11th, the day the chimney caught fire, the doctor had rushed in asking to use the telephone. Petiot had a loud and booming voice, and it did not require much effort on the part of the *patron* to hear that Petiot was talking to his brother Maurice in Auxerre. 'Burn all the papers!' he heard him say. He then rushed out of the café.

The next day Petiot took his bewildered wife and child to Auxerre, where the family spent the night with Maurice.

171

The following morning he returned to Paris alone and went into hiding at the flat of a former patient, a 56-year-old house-painter called Georges Redoute who lived in the St Denis area. Here he maintained a very low profile for several weeks, growing a beard and explaining to his somewhat simple friend that he had to be hidden in disguise for fear of the Gestapo finding out what he had been doing to aid the Resistance.

The newspapers, meanwhile, were having a field-day with details of the findings at the rue Le Sueur and Petiot's disappearance. Discreet enquiries at the Gestapo H.Q. indicated that the Germans knew nothing of the doctor and his activities, information that was palpably false. Reporters interviewed friends, relatives and patients to build up a background story, and perhaps it was just as well that Mme Petiot and brother Maurice were placed under protective custody.

Well into 1944, persistent rumours of an intended Allied landing in France gradually drove the Petiot affair off the front pages. On 6th June the Normandy landings began, and Paris was liberated by the French army under General Leclerc on 24th August. Not until then did the press return to the mystery of the rue Le Sueur and the topic of Petiot's disappearance.

By any standards a bizarre case, it stimulated a great deal of correspondence in the press. But only one letter defended Petiot. This was received by a newspaper *La Resistance* and was signed 'A still-serving officer of the Resistance'. In it the anonymous correspondent said that even if Petiot had been a murderer, all his deeds were for the glory of France and the Resistance. He should be given a medal, the letter continued, rather than being hounded like a criminal, and one day the truth would be revealed.

The editor, astutely considering that this letter was very probably from Petiot himself, sent it on to the police. It was handwritten, and it did not take very long to compare it with the doctor's known writing and to decide that it was indeed from him.

But this brought them no nearer to establishing Petiot's whereabouts. They had heard rumours that he might have tried to join the Resistance under a false name after the Normandy Landings, and, without very much hope, started the laborious task of checking the handwriting with that of all officers known to have joined the Resistance since 6th June. To their surprise the check took only a few days. The writing proved to be identical with that of a Captain Witterwald who had joined the Resistance in July, and was at present serving in a unit at Reuilly.

'Captain Witterwald' was traced to a house-painter's flat in St Denis. The Resistance took him into custody at the end of October, and after identifying him as Petiot handed him over to the police on 2nd November 1944.

The *juge d'instruction* in the Petiot case was a M. Gollety. By the time he had completed his examination of witnesses and reviewed all the police evidence, eighteen months had passed and he had accumulated a mass of documents weighing almost seventy pounds. On 18th March 1946 Dr Marcel Petiot stood trial at the Assizes of the *département* of Seine charged with twenty-seven murders at the rue Le Sueur. He was defended by France's most famous lawyer, maître Floriot.

In court Petiot acted as the born showman he was. He dressed smartly every day, beaming and smiling at the jury in the initial stages of the trial. His defence, that all his victims were German soldiers or collaborators, and that he was also running an official escape route on behalf of the Resistance, was soon torn to shreds. By this time the war had been over for some time and it might have been expected that at least some of those he had assisted to 'escape' would have been in touch with their relatives in France. But witness

173

after witness went into the box and told their sad story. Nothing had ever been heard again of those unfortunates who had gone to 21 rue Le Sueur. In addition, many identified the belongings of their relatives, or goods they had forwarded to Petiot for onward transmission to South America or other places said to be their final destination.

Petiot's supposed association with the Resistance was proved equally false. He could name none of the Resistance leaders except for five who had been shot during the course of the war. Ex-Resistance officers, some of high rank, came into the box and gave evidence of the detailed organization of the movement. Yet none had heard of Petiot, nor of the group he said he had led. They maintained that the disposal of traitors in the manner described by Petiot would never have been carried out by a group acting independently, or, if it had, would surely have come to the knowledge of the organization. Nor did they have any information of a group led by Petiot arranging an escape route — knowledge of which would have been of vital importance to the Resistance.

In the dock, Petiot blustered and shouted at the three judges and at the jury. 'You know your duty,' he screamed. 'I did it all for France, and as true Frenchmen you must acquit me!'

Maître Floriot did his best, but the odds were overwhelmingly against him.

The trial lasted sixteen days, during which more than eighty prosecution witnesses were heard. At the end the jury took just over two hours to bring in a verdict of guilty in respect of twenty-four of the twenty-seven murders with which Petiot was charged. On hearing the verdict Petiot screamed at the jury in rage, and shouted at his wife, 'You must avenge me!'

Maître Floriot immediatley entered a pleas for Presidential clemency, but this was rejected.

Very early on the morning of Saturday, 26th May 1946, maître Floriot entered the condemned cell of the famous Santé prison in Paris and told his client that he was to be guillotined at 5 a.m. Petiot took the news calmly, pausing only to dress himself in his best suit and to write a letter to his wife and son. Just before five o'clock he set out on the long walk from the condemned cell to the guillotine, accompanied by Floriot, M. Gollety, the Advocate General and various prison officials including the Governor.

He refused a last drink in his cell, and also refused to take the last rites in the small chapel they passed on the way. But, for the sake of his wife, he did allow the chaplain to say a prayer for the repose of his soul. Finally, after a last cigarette which he did not finish, his hands were tied behind his back and his collar loosened. As the little group gathered closely round him he placed his head ready on the block. With terrible and silent efficiency the blade descended.

9

Robert George Clements
(1880-1947)

Some multiple murderers, like the notorious Dr Neill Cream, are remarkable for their arrogance. This manifestation of conceit springs from a conviction that they can easily hoodwink the police no matter how many clues are strewn in their path, coupled with a desire to flaunt their expertise before the general public.

Dr Robert George Clements was a multiple murderer, yet very unlike Cream. True, he was a flamboyant and extrovert man, but in matters of murder he preferred to commit his crimes quietly and to benefit from a loophole in the law: i.e. that it is perfectly legal for a physician in Britain to treat his wife if she is ill, and also to sign the death certificate without recourse to another doctor. It is, of course, contrary to the ethical code of the British Medical Association, and a doctor discovered doing this today would almost certainly be reprimanded. But the rules of the B.M.A. are not the laws of England − a fact which Clements (and possibly others before and since) used to his advantage.

Irishmen are popularly supposed to be gifted with irresistable powers of persuasion. Whether or not he had actually been suspended by his heels to kiss the famous stone at Blarney Castle, Robert George Clements, born in Limerick in 1880, was no exception to the rule. During his lifetime he persuaded four women to marry him, and three of them to part with their not inconsiderable fortunes. With his blarney he coerced a young doctor into certifying a false cause of death in respect of his fourth wife, and so precipitated his own demise and that of his colleague.

Clements is the only British doctor to have been convicted of murder this century (Crippen was neither a doctor nor British, and Buck Ruxton was a Parsee Indian), but even so he was never brought to trial in a court of law, but convicted by a coroner's jury. Like many multiple murderers before him, Clements eventually became careless, murdering his fourth wife in the same town, Southport, where his third wife had died in suspicious circumstances only eight years previously.

Clements was a big, bluff Irishman who had qualified as an M.D. in Belfast in 1904, when he was twenty-four. He was already developing a paunch and a tendency to pomposity that was to remain with him for the rest of his life. He was undoubtedly attracted to the swinging social life of Belfast, and liked to be seen in the best restaurants, attending the theatre and escorting pretty women. But all this took money, and as a comparatively impecunious general practitioner he had difficulty in maintaining this kind of lifestyle. He decided that the obvious thing to do, since he himself did not have the means, was to marry someone with plenty of money and who enjoyed the social round as much as he did.

He was a good, some said brilliant, doctor, and in 1912 took his F.R.C.S. examination. That same year he married Edyth Ann Mercier, a somewhat plain woman ten years older than himself, but with the distinct advantage of having a father who was an immensely wealthy Belfast corn- and grain-merchant. In this first marriage Clements was decidedly fortunate. Not only did Mr Mercier settle a very large sum on his daughter at the time of her marriage, but he died eighteen months later leaving Edyth another £25,000 in his will. He was a patient of Clements, who certified death as being due to cancer.

Clements and his wife were popular members of Belfast

society, and lived well. They occupied a large detached house in one of the more prestigious suburbs of the city, and joined the local music society and several other associations. It soon became apparent that the doctor had an eye for the ladies and his philanderings and somewhat unsubtle attempts at flirtations were noted by many of the women in the circles in which they moved.

Edyth, though she was probably aware of her husband's roving eye, did not seem to mind too much and did not take the matter seriously. Unprepossessing and totally devoid of glamour, at forty-two years of age she seemed only too pleased to have a husband who was so popular, even if he was spending her money at a rapid rate.

It took just eight years to dissipate her fortune and early in 1920, she discovered there were only a few hundred pounds left in the joint account. She remonstrated with her husband, but her financial worries were overshadowed by the onset of a serious illness, described by her husband as 'sleeping sickness'. This is a tropical disease for which there is very little hope of a cure. Clements himself voiced this opinion from the onset and told friends that it was 'only a matter of time'. He was correct, and Edyth Clements died in the autumn of 1920. The doctor signed the death certificate himself, and after the funeral was over sold his practice, left Belfast and moved to Manchester. Here he established himself once more as a general practitioner and was engaged in the same sort of social round to which he had been accustomed in Belfast. He joined several clubs, became a Freemason and was seen in all the best places, usually escorting pretty women, particularly if they happened to be wealthy widows or the daughters of well-to-do parents.

He married for the second time in the summer of 1921, his bride on this occasion being Mary McCleery, the daughter of a rich Manchester industrialist whose family, like that of Clements, originally hailed from Ireland.

After his marriage the pattern of living for the doctor resumed its course, though this time the second Mrs Clements was more critical of her husband's roving eye and philanderings. She, too, had had a large sum of money settled on her at marriage, but their life-style was such that it only lasted four years. As the money dwindled, Mary was reported by her husband to be suffering from a heart complaint and in 1925 she died suddenly, her husband attending her and furnishing a certificate giving endocarditis as the cause of death.

For the next two years Clements vanished from the scene. He went to sea as a ship's doctor and travelled extensively in the Orient, returning in 1927 complete with a Japanese manservant, which caused a certain amount of surprise when he set up practice in Manchester once again.

There he reverted to his old ways as a medical Don Juan and became friendly with several wealthy women. But on this occasion he did not run true to form. In 1928 he married for the third time, but his choice was not a woman of wealth but an old family friend, Katherine Burke, who had known both his previous wives. Of his increasing collection of spouses, Katherine seems to be the only one who was not wealthy and one must therefore assume that in this instance it was a genuine love-match.

The doctor had been assiduously feathering his own nest, and with a successful practice he was able to keep up his normal life-style as long as he was reasonably careful. It was about this time that Clements became interested in what today is termed 'fringe medicine' and experimented with hydrotherapy and herbalism, as well as investigating the advantages or otherwise of the accepted continental practice of giving almost all medicine by means of suppositories or anal douches.

In 1933 Clements, by then fifty-three, decided to go into semi-retirement. He and Katherine moved south and for two years ran a hotel at Bransgore, in the New Forest. This was not a great success, for Katherine's health was not of the best and, with her husband frequently away doing locum work, she found she had to bear most of the responsibility of running the hotel. In addition she did not like the south of England, and in 1935 they sold the hotel and returned north, this time to live in Southport.

Here the couple were as popular as ever and they renewed contact with many friends in Manchester. They seemed happy enough, but by 1938 Katherine's small capital was almost gone and the money they spent came from Clements's own earnings. Fond as he was of Katherine, this was not the situation that Clements had in mind, and from that time on his wife's life was in jeopardy. She died early in 1939, and on this occasion a local practitioner was called in to sign the death certificate. Clements suggested strongly that his wife had died of tuberculosis, and, indeed, for some weeks he had been telling friends of her failing health and prophesying her death almost to the very day. The death certificate was signed accordingly.

One of Katherine's closest friends in Southport had been a lady doctor called Irene Gayus. She was not one to fall for charm, and, in fact, disliked Clements intensely. From friends in Manchester she learned of the deaths of Clements's two previous wives when their money had gone. During Katherine's illness she became very suspicious of the doctor, particularly when she discovered that the death certificate of both previous wives had been signed by the doctor himself. She also knew that during the weeks immediately prior to the death of her friend, Clements had been having an open affair with a very wealthy woman in the town.

Dr Gayus's discoveries disturbed her deeply, and on the death of the third Mrs Clements she immediately sought out the Chief Constable of Southport, Lt.-Col. Harold Mighall, and voiced her fears and suspicions. The Chief Constable thought the matter serious enough to warrant some action on his part, and after consultation with the coroner ordered a post-mortem. Unfortunately he was a few hours too late, and Katherine Clements had already been cremated in Liverpool in the presence of her husband and sorrowing relatives.

Whether or not Clements was aware of these misgivings on the part of Dr Gayus is not clear, but at all events he does not seem to have wished to remain a widower for long. Less than twelve months after the death of his third wife he was actively courting Amy Victoria Barnett, another Southport lady of means, this time twenty years his junior. Her father was a Liverpool industrial tycoon and Managing Director of the Liverpool Cartage Company. He died unexpectedly in January 1940, leaving his daughter £22,000 as her share of his fortune, and in June 1940 Amy Barnett (or 'Vee' as she preferred to be called) had the doubtful distinction of becoming the fourth Mrs Clements.

In 1940 wartime restrictions had scarcely had time to be felt, and the wedding was an extremely opulent affair at St George's, Hanover Square, in London, with a reception for several hundred guests at the Mayfair Hotel. The happy couple then returned to the luxurious flat on the North Promenade at Southport, formerly occupied by the father of the bride.

Clements, a wealthy man once more, did not need to work full-time, but in those first few months of 'the phoney war' he took a job as consultant M.D. at the Kenworthy Hydro, Southport. Later, as more doctors joined the Services, he was appointed deputy Medical Officer of Health for Blackburn, and did the journey daily back and forth from Southport.

At home the couple appeared to be a most devoted pair and joined in many activities in the district. Vee was a talented pianist and musician and had several of her compositions published at her own expense. Both were very keen on amateur theatricals, and Mrs Clements was a staunch worker for Christ Church, Southport, where her husband was a sidesman. Clements himself was a member of various associations including the Friends of Czechoslovakia and the European Aid Society. He had risen to some prominence in the Masonic movement and was an active member of the local Conservative party. From time to time he contributed papers to the *Lancet* and the *British Medical Journal*.

The drama surrounding the almost inevitable death of the fourth Mrs Clements began in December 1946 when a local physician and Chairman of the medical board of Southport Infirmary, Dr John Holmes, was called in by Clements to examine his wife. According to her husband she was suffering from violent headaches, giddiness and loss of memory, which was causing him concern. Apart from what Dr Holmes was later to describe as 'symptoms of nervous illness' he could find nothing organically wrong with Vee, and said so. On discussing her condition with Clements the latter made the suggestion that she might be suffering from a tumour on the brain, but Dr Holmes discounted this.

By February 1947 Mrs Clements seemed much improved and was out and about again, and it was therefore with some surprise that Dr Holmes discovered that Clements was telling friends in Manchester that his wife was still very ill and that it was 'only a matter of time'. Once again the sinister prophecies were beginning.

On the evening of the 26th May Clements telephoned Dr Holmes and told him his wife was dying and asked him to get her into a nursing home as soon as possible. Dr Holmes accordingly arranged for her to enter the Astley Bank Nursing Home in Southport where she was admitted in a comatose condition later that night. In the meantime Clements had telephoned a friend of his, a wealthy widow called

Mrs Stevens, and arranged to lodge with her while his wife was in hospital.

The superintendent of the nursing home was Dr Andrew Brown, and as soon as Mrs Clements was admitted he examined her in the company of the matron, Mrs Baxendale, and Dr Holmes, who had accompanied the patient. Dr Brown immediately noticed that Mrs Clements's eyes had pin-point pupils. Mrs Baxendale said, 'It looks more like morphine poisoning to me than cerebral trouble.' Dr Brown agreed.

Mrs Clements's skin was also beginning to take on a bluish tinge and she had difficulty with her breathing. All the symptoms pointed to morphine over-dosage and before he left the nursing home Dr Brown gave strict instructions to the matron that under no circumstances should morphine in any form be given to the patient, even if prescribed by Dr Holmes.

Mrs Clements remained unconscious throughout the night and died at 9.30 the following morning. Clements was told and immediately began talking of cerebral tumour being the cause of death. Dr Brown, from what he had seen of the patient, was extremely doubtful of this. He told Clements that he wished to conduct a post-mortem examination on his wife, and to examine the brain, and to this Clements agreed. The post-mortem was arranged immediately at the nursing home, without reference to the coroner or anyone else. For this action Dr Brown was to be severely criticized later.

To conduct this post-mortem Dr Brown requested the assistance of Dr James Houston, a young pathologist at Southport Infirmary, who attended the nursing home and carried out the examination in the room in which Mrs Clements had died. Houston also came from Northern Ireland and was a friend of the Clements's. He was a brilliant pathologist and an extremely conscientious man, indeed, something of a perfectionist.

183

He duly removed the brain of the dead woman but found no evidence of any kind indicating a cerebral tumour. Dr Brown's suspicions increased and he instructed Dr Houston to continue and to carry out a full post-mortem. For the next two hours Houston worked at this task, removing several organs in the process. He was primarily a haematologist, and there is evidence that Clements had hinted to him that his wife was suffering from myeloid leukaemia. At all events he took samples of blood back with him to the laboratory for further and more detailed examination.

For some reason that has never been explained he also instructed the laboratory technician who was with him to destroy all the organs he had removed during the autopsy, though he had not examined any of them microscopically. Later that day Houston reported that the blood smear he had examined confirmed the existence of myeloid leukaemia, and he signed the death certificate to that effect.

The suspicious Dr Brown was far from happy at this turn of events. He decided to seek out the coroner for the area, Mr C. Bolton. The coroner in turn passed on the information to the Chief Constable, the same Lt.-Col. Harold Mighall who had attempted to stop the funeral of the third Mrs Clements eight years before.

The police had been interested in Dr Clements ever since that time, and in the light of these latest developments acted extremely quickly. They interviewed the Clements's charlady, a Mrs Keefe, who said that Mrs Clements had frequently lapsed into unconsciousness, but that her husband always seemed to know when these episodes were about to occur, and always told her not to come in the day before. Mrs Keefe also said that Mrs Clements's complexion had gradually been turning yellow for several weeks and that most of the time she seemed incapable of doing any work around the house, which was in a shocking condition despite all the efforts of Mrs Keefe herself.

Another friend of Mrs Clements said that the doctor had tried to stop her having any contact with his wife, and at the end had had the telephone removed so that she could not even talk to her.

But, most sinister of all, the local C.I.D. discovered that Clements had been writing prescriptions for large quantities of morphine sulphate tablets for various patients who did not need them, and indeed were quite unaware they had been prescribed, for they had never had them.

The Chief Constable thereupon decided to act – and act quickly. On the morning of the funeral, with the mourners already gathered at the church, he gave instructions that the service should be postponed and the body removed for a second post-mortem. Dr Houston was also advised of this development and became extremely agitated. He said 'My God, I wish I had known about this before.'

The police then hurried to Clements's flat but found him unconscious in the kitchen. He died a few hours later at the Infirmary of what was decided later to be a self-inflicted injection of morphine. In the flat he left a note which said: 'To whom it may concern – I can no longer tolerate this diabolical insult to me.'

The second post-mortem on the fourth Mrs Clements was undertaken by Dr Grace, a Home Office pathologist. In the absence of most of the vital organs he was able to certify only that death was definitely not due to myeloid leukaemia. Assistance was requested from Dr J.B. Firth, Director of the Home Office Forensic Laboratory at Preston. He had little enough to work on, but carried out tests on part of the kidney, a small amount of muscle, and a short section of spine weighing less than an ounce round the site of which there appeared to be the mark of an injection. With this small amount of material Dr Firth conducted difficult and exhaustive tests during the next fortnight, finally establishing without doubt that the organs at his disposal reacted positively to

185

the presence of morphine, and that this had almost certainly been the cause of death. The amounts he reported were 1.34 milligrams of morphine in the kidney and 0.8 milligrams in the spine. In his opinion this represented a very high original injection of the substance.

In the course of his duties Dr Firth, in company with the police, had examined the North Promenade flat in which the Clements had lived. They found it in a state of indescribable confusion and filth. Groceries which had gone rancid were stacked high in the kitchen, the bedclothes consisted only of blankets which were almost black with dirt, and coal was piled everywhere, even under the kitchen table. But even more significant was the discovery of dozens of bottles of tablets in almost every room, some of them empty but some containing tablets and labelled 'phenobarbitone, one to be taken night and morning.' The labels showed the name of the local pharmacy and the code number for a private prescription, but the significant fact was that the bottles did not actually contain phenobarbitone tablets, but ¾-grain tablets of morphine sulphate. It was obvious that Mrs Clements had been given morphine tablets over a very long period.

The mystery of the death of Mrs Clements, followed so dramatically by the death of her husband, caused a major sensation. But an even greater sensation occurred a few days later when, on 2nd June, Dr Houston was found dead in his laboratory at Southport Infirmary. He had committed suicide by taking over 300 times the lethal dose of sodium cyanide. He had also left a note which read:

'I have for some time been aware that I have been making mistakes. I have not profited by my experience. I was convinced that Mrs Clements died of leukaemia, and accordingly destroyed the vital organs after completing my autopsy.'

For many people the most tragic part of this extraordinary affair was the death of Dr Houston, a brilliant pathologist and popular with his colleagues, happily married with two children. His wife was later to say that for some time he seemed to be suffering from the strain of overwork, so much so that she had written to his parents expressing fears about his health and the almost over-conscientious way in which he performed his duties.

His colleagues showed the greatest sympathy for Dr Houston and regretted the tragic end to such a brilliant career. Dr Cronin Lowe, honorary consultant pathologist to Southport Infirmary said of him,

'My opinion is that Dr Houston's diagnosis of myeloid leukaemia was an honest and genuine one but based on insufficient evidence. In some inexplicable way his usually careful mental approach to a problem had been biased. When, later, he discovered that there were other features surrounding the case of which he was not aware, he had only to say that he wished to revise his previous diagnosis and opinion. Unfortunately, being of a reserved and reticent nature, he did not confide in those who would gladly have helped him, and took this most regrettable step which closed a highly specialised and brilliant professional career.'

On Tuesday 25th June, 1947 the triple inquest on Mrs Clements, Dr Clements and Dr Houston was opened by the Southport coroner, Mr Bolton.

The affair had created much national and even international interest. The coroner expressed criticism of some newspapers who, he said, had sent reporters to Southport 'with wallets stuffed with money' ready to pay for any titbits of information from any person who had even a nodding acquaintance with the Clements. He warned the jury, and the public for that matter, that any reports purporting to reflect either his opinion or the opinions of the police should be totally disregarded until the inquest was over and the verdicts returned.

He was also somewhat critical of the action of Dr Brown in ordering the original autopsy on Mrs Clements without any reference to him, and commented adversely on the fact that a full post-mortem had been conducted in the bedroom where the patient died, and not at the Infirmary, where it should have been conducted.

One odd feature of the police evidence turned on the contents of Dr Clements's diaries that had been found in the flat. Mrs Clements had actually died in the Astley Bank Nursing Home at 9.30 in the morning, but Clements had recorded her death as having taken place at 9.15 a.m. Even odder was the fact that, according to a family friend, the doctor had telephoned him at 5 minutes to 9 that morning to tell him that his wife was already dead!

In addition there was a great deal of discrepancy between Clements's account of his wife's illness and the evidence brought by various friends of Mrs Clements. From the previous December, when Dr Holmes had first attended her, Clements had constantly been referring to his wife's increasing disorientation and lassitude, though some friends claimed that the couple were seen regularly dining at a Lord Street restaurant and that Mrs Clements seemed perfectly normal. Clements told one friend that they usually dined out because Mrs Clements was such a poor housekeeper, and since their marriage he had hardly had one cooked meal at home. This seems to be borne out by the shocking state of the North Promenade flat.

Another abnormality centred on the statement in Clements's diary covering the evening immediately prior to his wife's death. In this he said,

'Set out for a walk in the afternoon. Tea at home. After tea went for walk to the Post Office. Vee commenced to lose voice and the power of her limbs. Got her home with difficulty and with a fearful headache. After washing-up found her unconscious. Sent for Dr Holmes.'

He also said that at one point Mrs Clements had collapsed on the promenade. Yet according to the evidence of a lynx-eyed neighbour, the Clements had certainly gone for a walk that evening, but had returned arm-in-arm at 10.15, laughing and joking on the doorstep while the doctor looked for his key. There was certainly no question of Mrs Clements having to be assisted into the house.

The coroner reminded the jury that all the medical evidence available agreed that there was no organic disease present that could have caused Mrs Clements to lapse into unconsciousness at frequent intervals. 'Does it not seem strange,' he said, 'that a woman with no obvious organic disease should apparently be well at 10.15 but that she should be unconscious and dying within the next hour?'

The coroner also pointed out to the jury that the apparent lack of motive for Clements to kill his wife was immaterial. If they thought it was a wilful act on his part they should return a verdict accordingly.

As regards the death of Dr Clements himself, he wished to be as fair as possible to a man who was no longer present and in a position to defend himself or explain his actions. His death was either *felo de se*, or self-murder, or alternatively suicide while of unsound mind. Did he, perhaps, realize at the last moment that an act of murder he had committed had come to the knowledge of the police? Did he realize that the net was closing round him and was it in order to avoid the course of justice that he took his own life?

In the case of Dr Houston similar conditions prevailed, except that it was known he had a history of depression long before he conducted the first autopsy on Mrs Clements, enough to cause his wife extreme anxiety. In view of these facts the jury might consider that Dr Houston took his own life whilst his mind was disturbed.

The coroner took the opportunity of thanking the police for their rapid action in investigating the death of Mrs

Clements, and in particular congratulated Dr Firth, the pathologist, on the difficult task he had performed in conducting an examination on such very sparse material.

The inquest had taken three days, and the jury returned the following verdicts:

1. Mrs Clements was murdered by Dr Clements.
2. Dr Clements committed *felo de se*.
3. Dr Houston took his life while the balance of his mind was disturbed.

As the main culprit was now dead the police decided to take no further action in the matter of the deaths of the three previous wives, which, in any case, had taken place so long before.

There still remains the question of motive. Clements undoubtedly killed his first two wives when their money ran out and may very possibly have killed his third wife when his own finances became strained. But with Vee, money does not seem to have been the motive, for Mrs Clements left £51,000 gross when she died, and Clements left £12,000 in his will. Despite the inconsistencies in his diary there were plenty of people to say that for most of their married life Mrs Clements was well, and the couple seemed fond of each other and happy. Clements did not appear to have any obvious motive for getting rid of his wife unless he had tired of her and, like Edward Pritchard and many others before him, saw his wife as a barrier to further amorous conquests.

Clements was undoubtedly a wily bird, but in the end a careless one. He does not seem to have studied sufficiently the subject of murder by morphine. Had he done so he would have known of the case of Dr Buchanan of New York in 1892, who also murdered his wife by this means. But Buchanan adopted a more scientific approach and while he was administering the poison was also instilling atropine into his wife's eyes, which had the effect of dilating the pupils and masking the characteristic pin-points which denote the presence of morphine.

An an appendix to the Clements case a question was asked in the House of Commons by the Member for Stockport on 3rd July 1947: 'In view of a recent case at Southport, was the Minister of Health aware that the law permitted medical practitioners to issue death certificates in respect of close relatives, and if he proposed legislation to end this practice?'

The Minister, Mr Aneurin Bevan, said in reply that he was not contemplating any change in the law.

Britain still remains almost the only country in the civilized world where a doctor may issue a death certificate in respect of his own family, and, unless there is another 'Clements case', it seems likely to remain that way.

10

Sam Sheppard

(1924-1970)

From time to time a country experiences a *cause célèbre* which has the effect of dividing the community into two opposing factions. Lifelong friends develop violently differing views on the case, strangers come to blows discussing it, and breaches are created amongst members of the same family that are sometimes never healed. In 1890 Britain was split in two over the case of Charles Parnell and Kitty O'Shea, while France was fundamentally divided by *l'affaire Dreyfus* at the turn of the century. In America public opinion was equally divided over the case of Sam Sheppard in 1954.

Had Dr Sam Sheppard not been quite such a successful member of his profession, had he not been so wealthy and handsome, and had he not been proved to be something of a philanderer, the case might have taken a very different course. As it was, his social status, his private life and the support of his well-to-do family created an atmosphere of class-consciousness which, fanned by accusations and innuendos from the local and national press, engendered a feeling of hostility towards the doctor from the start and virtually convicted him before his trial.

In addition, the facts as described by Sheppard himself were by no means clear-cut and there was more than one interpretation of his version of the events of the night of 3rd July 1954 — the night that his pregnant wife Marilyn was found bludgeoned to death in her bedroom while her husband was present in the house.

Sam Sheppard was a wealthy and successful osteopath and

chiropractor, thirty years old, good-looking, married and with one child, a boy of seven. With his two older brothers and his father (all doctors) he was a partner in the fashionable family-owned 100-bed Bay View Hospital in the suburb of Bay Village near Cleveland, Ohio. His house, on the shores of Lake Erie, was elegant and expensive as befitted a young doctor already estimated to be earning upwards of $45,000 a year. Nine years previously he had married his childhood sweetheart, Marilyn, whom he apparently adored. To all outward appearances the Sheppards were the blueprint for the ideal American couple and a living manifestation of the Great American Dream.

A little after five o'clock on the afternoon of Saturday, 3rd July 1954, Dr Sheppard arrived home from the clinic in his smart new Jaguar. His wife met him at the door, and reminded him that they had invited their near neighbours, Mr and Mrs Don Ahern, for dinner that evening; it had been arranged that the Sheppards would go round to the Aherns for pre-dinner cocktails. Dr Sam was not all that pleased at the reminder. He had come home early that day ready to mow the lawn in preparation for a party the Sheppards were holding the next day, Sunday, to celebrate the Fourth of July. However, in view of the arrangements, he put off this scheme and, after washing and changing, accompanied his wife to the Aherns, driving there in his second and larger car, a Lincoln Convertible.

After several drinks and general chat the two families moved back to the Sheppard house for dinner, Marilyn going ahead to check that all was in order for the meal.

The evening went smoothly, though Sam Sheppard seemed rather tired after a busy week at the clinic. After the meal had ended and Marilyn had put their son, Chip, to bed, the two couples settled down: Nancy Ahern and Marilyn watched a television play in the lounge while Sam and Don Ahern listened to a baseball match on the radio in the kitchen. After the match ended the two men moved into the lounge and Marilyn sat on her husband's lap, with her arms round him, watching the end of the play. A little while later the doctor said he was feeling sleepy and stretched himself out on the couch where he eventually fell asleep.

Soon after midnight the Aherns decided to leave and were shown out by Marilyn, tiptoeing gently across the room past the sleeping Sam. They left by the door most often used by the family – the side-door facing the lake – and Marilyn, after emptying the ashtrays and tidying up, went up to bed, leaving her husband asleep on the couch. At the time he was wearing slacks, a T-shirt and a jacket.

What happened during the next few hours is wrapped in mystery, but it resulted in Marilyn Sheppard being battered to death with nearly forty blows from some heavy instrument, and Dr Sam Sheppard later being indicted for murder.

His own account of what happened that night is, of necessity, hazy, for according to him, he was twice knocked unconscious by an assailant, sustaining injuries to his face and neck. In his statement to the police he said that he was dimly conscious of the departure of the Aherns and Marilyn going up to bed. Some time later (he had no idea how long) he was aroused by screams from his wife's room. His statement continued:

> At this time I was on the couch. I think that she cried or screamed my name once or twice, during which time I ran upstairs, thinking that she might be having a reaction similar to convulsions she had in the early days of her pregnancy.
>
> I charged into our room and saw a form with a light garment, I believe, at the same time grappling with something or someone. During this short period I could hear loud moans or groaning sounds and noises. I was struck down. It seems like I was hit from behind somehow but had grappled with this individual from in front or gen-

erally in front of me. I was apparently knocked out. The next thing I know I was gathering my senses while coming to a sitting position next to the bed, my feet towards the hallway.

He then described how he looked at the figure of his wife on the bed and decided she was dead. He checked that young Chip was safe and came back to the hallway.

After this I thought I heard a noise downstairs, seemingly in the front eastern portion of the house. I went downstairs as rapidly as I could, coming down the west division of the steps. I then saw a form progressing rapidly somewhere between the door towards the lake and the screen door, or possibly slightly beyond the screen door.

I pursued this form through the door, over the porch, and out the screen door — all the doors were evidently open — down the steps to the beach-house landing, and then on down the steps to the beach, where I lunged or jumped and grasped him in some manner from the back, either body or leg, it was something solid. However, I am not sure. This was beyond the steps, an unknown distance, but probably about ten feet. I had the feeling of twisting, or choking and this terminated my consciousness.

The next thing I knew I came to a very groggy recollection of being at the water's edge on my face, being wallowed back and forth by the waves. My head was towards the bank, my legs and feet were towards the water. I staggered to my feet and slowly came to some sort of sense. I don't know how long it took but I staggered up the stairs towards the house and at some time came to the realization that something was wrong and that my wife had been injured.

I went back upstairs and looked at my wife and felt her and checked her pulse on her neck and determined or felt that she was gone. I became or thought that I was disorientated and the victim of a bizarre dream and I believe I paced in and out of the room and possibly into one of the other rooms. I may have re-examined her, finally realizing that this was true.

I went downstairs. I believe I went through the kitchen door into my study, searching for a name, a number, or what to do. A number came to me and I called it, believing that this number was Mr Houk's. I don't remember what I said to Mr Houk. He and his wife arrived shortly afterwards.

The Mr Houk Sam telephoned was J. Spencer Houk, the Mayor of Bay Village and a close friend of the Sheppards. Though the doctor could not remember what he said, or at what time he made the call, Houk was to testify that the call from Sheppard came through at 5.45 a.m., and that Sheppard said, 'My God, Spence, get over here quick. I think they've killed Marilyn. Get over here quick.'

Houk reached the Sheppard house with his wife within minutes. There they found the door on the lake side of the house unlocked, with the doctor sitting slumped in his den, naked to the waist, with his trousers wringing wet. Houk asked him what had happened, and he replied, 'I don't exactly know, but somebody ought to do something for Marilyn.' Mrs Houk decided to go upstairs to see what had happened to her friend, but within seconds of seeing the bludgeoned and blood-stained corpse was shouting to her husband to send for a doctor and call the police.

This Houk did, and the police arrived at 6.00 a.m., followed within minutes by Dr Richard Sheppard, one of Sam's brothers, who had also been informed. His was the first professional examination of the body, and he estimated that death had taken place not more than two hours previously. Later that morning at about 8 a.m., the County Coroner, Dr Samuel Gerber, examined the body and according to his findings, death had taken place between 3 a.m., and 4 a.m. This question of the apparent time of death was destined to be of paramount importance later, when the prosecution was to allege that the two or three hours between the murder and Sam's call to the Houks was spent by him arranging things to look as if an intruder had been on the premises.

The first policeman to arrive at the house was 28-year-old Patrolman Drenkhan of the Bay Village Police Department, of which he had been a member for four years. He knew Sam Sheppard well, and had been with him on several road accident cases in the past, as Sheppard was also police surgeon for the area. Before leaving his office, Drenkhan had already called for an ambulance and advised his immediate superior, Police Chief John Eaton.

Drenkhan's first act on arriving at the house was to go upstairs to the bedroom. In the room were two four-poster beds separated by a small bedside-table and lamp. Sam's bed was undisturbed, though with several drops of blood on the coverlet. On the other bed lay the body of Marilyn Sheppard, her face smashed in and covered with blood. The top of her pyjamas had been pulled up under her arms, leaving her chest exposed, and a sheet covered her legs. The pillow, mattress and bedclothes were soaked in blood.

Having viewed the scene, Drenkhan went downstairs and asked the doctor what had happened. Sheppard told him he had heard screams, had fought with someone on the stairs and then chased him into the lake. He had lost consciousness at the water's edge and on recovery had come back into the house and gone upstairs again.

Drenkhan told Houk, who was still with Sheppard, that the matter was 'too big for us' and Houk advised him to notify the coroner. By this time the ambulance, fireman and several more police were on the scene, to be joined shortly by Police Chief Eaton.

By 6.20 the eldest Sheppard brother, Stephen, had

197

arrived, and he and Richard went into conference to decide what their next move should be. Their decision was to be a controversial one, for by 6.30 they had arranged for the still-confused Sam to be put into the ambulance and transported to their own Bay View Hospital. Though permission for this had not been requested, Police Chief Eaton raised no objection.

During the hours that followed, various members of the Cleveland homicide department arrived, including a fingerprint expert, and just before eight o'clock the coroner, Dr Sam Gerber, made his appearance and apparently took control of the matter. Needless to say the press had been alerted, and neighbours and children were thronging the area, together with reporters, photographers and several other citizens of Bay Village and even further afield. It was the beginning of what was afterwards described as a 'Roman holiday atmosphere', an atmosphere which was to continue throughout the trial and which almost certainly influenced its result.

Dr Gerber, having first looked round the house and heard a brief account of the affair from those present, decided to go immediately to the hospital and question Sheppard officially. His story remained substantially the same, and Gerber eventually left the hospital taking with him Sheppard's slippers, his wet trousers, a pair of shorts and Sheppard's wallet. He then returned to the scene of the crime to find out what the Cleveland detectives had discovered.

The homicide squad had not been idle. They found that in the upper rooms of the house, apart from the bedroom, nothing had been disturbed. But downstairs there was considerable disorder. In Sheppard's office and in the dining-room drawers had been been pulled out of two bureaux and papers scattered everywhere, an ornament had been knocked over and smashed, and his medical bag lay in the hall with its contents strewn around. On the floor of the living-room lay Marilyn's watch with fresh blood adhering to the face and the wrist-strap.

On the face of it, the situation was consistent with a murderous attack by a burglar discovered in the act, but there were also some missing factors. For one thing, there was no sign of the murder weapon; and secondly there was the curious discovery by Grabowski, the finger-print expert, that nowhere in the house was there a single finger-print to be found. It looked suspiciously as if every surface had been deliberately wiped clean. There appeared to be no sign of forcible entry, though this could be accounted for by the fact that the lake door was rarely locked at night. An interesting point was that Sheppard's corduroy jacket was found neatly folded at the head of the couch, though he had been wearing it when he dozed off in the presence of his wife and the Aherns the evening before. Missing also was the T-shirt Sam had been wearing at the time.

The homicide men, led by Detective Robert Schottke, were not at all happy with these findings and decided to question Sheppard in hospital. The interview lasted just over twenty minutes, and was interrupted no fewer than four times by his brother Stephen, who seemed particularly anxious to supervise everything Sam was saying.

There were, in fact, discrepancies in the story Sheppard told the detectives. Originally he claimed to have been attacked at the top of the stairs, but now he told Schottke the attack had taken place in the bedroom. Though he had previously stated more than once that at no time had he seen more than a vague figure or outline of the figure he'd grappled with, he now told the detectives that he'd chased a tall, dark man wearing dark clothing. These variations could well be accounted for by the fact that he had been in a state of shock for some hours (it was by then nearly noon) but for the detectives it did little more than to underline their dissatisfaction with his version of events. It was becoming clear to them that Sheppard himself *could* have been the murderer, and they began probing for motive.

With the experience of some 15,000 murders a year in the United States the detectives were well aware that when a wife was found murdered a 'mysterious stranger' was frequently reported in the vicinity. It was also a fact that in many cases the husband himself proved to be the killer, and, in common with police the world over, in cases of wife-murder they immediately put the husband at the head of the list of suspects.

The most obvious motive for this type of murder is generally that the husband is having an affair with another woman. Schottke, in the few hours that had elapsed between the murder and his interviewing Sheppard had stumbled across such evidence. He began by asking him about his relationship with his wife, and then put it to him that rumours were current in the area that for some time the doctor had been sexually intimate with a pretty young laboratory assistant at the Bay View Hospital. Susan Hayes had been at the hospital for two years, but had then moved to Los Angeles. The rumours had it that Sam, visiting that city for a medical convention in March 1954, had renewed his acquaintance with Susan and had spent several nights with her.

Sheppard denied these allegations strenuously, and Schottke did not pursue them. The interview ended with Schottke telling Sheppard boldly that in his opinion, if in nobody else's, he had murdered his wife. To this Sheppard replied quietly, 'Don't be ridiculous. I have devoted my life to saving lives and I love my wife.'

Soon after this uncomfortable interview with the detectives, the wretched Sheppard had to undergo yet another examination. This, however, was a physical one arranged by Dr Gerber in an attempt to ascertain the extent of the neck and face injuries Sheppard had sustained. The examination was carried out by a local Bay Village physician, Dr Richard Hexter, assisted by a junior doctor. Hexter reported to Gerber that in their opinion it was quite possible that Sam's injuries could have been self-inflicted.

It was obvious from all this that both Gerber and the Cleveland police entertained grave doubts about Sheppard's innocence. Though no charges were brought at that moment, a policeman was stationed outside his room at the hospital until he was discharged a few days later. More serious was the impounding of the Sheppard home by the police and their retention of the keys. On hearing of the police suspicions, the Sheppard family called a conference and decided to hire a lawyer to protect Sam's interests. Arthur Petersilge, already legal representative of the hospital, brought in a Cleveland lawyer and family friend, William J. Corrigan, who had a wide experience in criminal cases.

The press, in the meantime, were having a field-day. From the outset there was no shortage of sources of information, for no less than five separate authorities, all unco-ordinated, were dealing with the case. There was the Bay Village Police Department under Chief Eaton; the homicide squad of the Cleveland police led by Detective Schottke; and Coroner Gerber's own department was also busy seeking and assembling evidence. In addition the local county sheriff and his deputies were working on the case, ably supported by the county prosecutor's office. It was not surprising, under these circumstances, that information and theories for the benefit of the press were available and it was generally accepted that these sources were mainly hostile to Sheppard and out to convict him.

The doctor's image was not improved by the contention in the press that the family had moved him out of the way to their own hospital within thirty minutes of the discovery of the murder. They conveniently ignored the fact that, far from being protected, Sheppard had undergone as much 'grilling' in hospital as he would have done in his own home.

The decision of the family to obtain legal advice at an early stage was also a subject of comment in the press, the implication being that it was very odd to obtain a lawyer for his defence even before he had been charged. It is quite true that at that point he had not been charged, but the family were well aware of what Schottke had said to Sam, and of the overall views of the police.

The worst condemnation in the press was centred round the figure of Susan Hayes, the former laboratory technician. She had been located in Los Angeles and had been questioned prior to the inquest called by Gerber on 21st July. At the inquest Sheppard denied that he had ever been intimate with Susan, though admitting that he had called on her while visiting Los Angeles. Unfortunately for Sheppard Susan had signed a deposition admitting sex with him at the hospital on various occasions during the two years she had been employed there, and on the nights he had been visiting Los Angeles.

At this revelation the newspapers, outwardly more shocked and outraged at this account of Sheppard's sexual aberrations than by the murder itself, accused the Bay Village police of 'covering up' for one of their most respected citizens, and demanded that Sheppard be arrested and charged forthwith. The Cleveland Police went into conference and made their decision.

On 30th July, at 10 p.m. Sheppard was arrested at the house of his father, where he had been living since his own house had been impounded by the police, and by midnight he had appeared at a brief court hearing at the County Hall where he was charged with the murder of his wife. He was immediately lodged in the county gaol without even being allowed to contact his lawyer.

Sheppard's arrest precipitated even greater excitement in

the Cleveland area. In the county gaol the police worked on him in an attempt to extract a confession. They failed. As well as the police, three doctors, including a neurologist, examined him frequently and he was subjected to what he afterwards described as a period of mental torture. The police used their well-tried method of 'blowing hot and cold' by grilling him in pairs, one officer being apparently kindly and sympathetic for a period, but immediately followed by another who shouted accusations at him and tried to break down his story.

They delved into his private life and attempted to prove that his relationship with his wife was unstable and that he had had affairs with many women. The police passed on these details to the press, who printed them gleefully, and at one point devoted much space to the subject of Sheppard's sexual relationship with a former nurse at the hospital. In the event the woman was located in Detroit and given a lie-detector test, which proved that this allegation was completely without foundation. But, though proved untrue, it was the sort of smear the public would remember and had its due effect in convicting Sam in the public mind.

William Corrigan, Sheppard's lawyer, finally managed to get a habeas corpus hearing on 16th August, but it was almost too late. After one day of freedom with his family, Sam was informed that a Grand Jury hearing had indicted him on a charge of murder in the first degree, and once again he was back in the county gaol.

For the next three months he was to be kept in prison, allowed access to his lawyers but all the while the subject of a campaign by the press that virtually accused him in print of killing his wife. Public opinion was being steadily stirred up against him and when the trial was finally fixed on 18th October, before Judge Edward Blythin, the first and most difficult task was to empanel a jury consisting of citizens unlikely to have been influenced by press and television reports.

William Corrigan, defending Sheppard, tried his best to achieve this objective by enquiring into the past history of every one of the panel of potential jurors, and raising objections to one after another. Two women were barred because they had worked in a hospital. Another man was objected to because he was employed at an agency owned by an uncle of the dead woman. It was discovered that one potential juryman was a postman who delivered mail to one of the prosecution lawyers — he was speedily sent on his way. In all, over sixty potential jurors were questioned and examined during the course of nearly two weeks before a jury of twelve, eight men and four women, was finally sworn in. Small wonder that Corrigan had initially pleaded with the judge that the trial venue should be changed to a court outside the county where the locals were less likely to be influenced against Sam. His request was refused.

After the empanelling of the jury another complication delayed the start of the trial. An anonymous telephone call to the court claimed that one of the chosen jurors had previously been convicted of indecency with a young male in a car, and was therefore not suitable. The matter was hurriedly investigated and found to be correct. The next twenty-four hours were spent by lawyers on both sides trying to devise a legal method of removing an already empanelled juror from the scene without having to start the selection process all over again. Finally a way was found, a substitute juror produced, and the trial proper commenced.

The State of Ohio had three prosecutors acting for them in the case, led by John J. Mahon, a man with twenty-two years' experience in criminal matters and a very able lawyer. In his opening remarks he expounded the case the prosecution would bring against Sam Sheppard, claiming that the accused had had a violent quarrel with his wife after the departure of the Aherns soon after midnight on 4th July, and had beaten her to death in the bedroom. The quarrel, said

Mahon, was about the other women in the doctor's life, and he said he would produce proof that Sheppard had been thinking of getting a divorce in order to marry Susan Hayes. According to Mahon there had never been any mysterious stranger on the premises, and in the hours between killing Marilyn and calling Spencer Houk, Sheppard had got rid of the weapon, probably in the lake, simulated a burglary and inflicted superficial wounds on himself.

The first prosecution witness was Dr Lester Adelson, the pathologist who had performed the autopsy on Marilyn Sheppard. He described her injuries in detail and showed the jury, on a portable screen, coloured slides of her battered face and head taken soon after she had been found. Sam Sheppard was unwilling to see these gory pictures, and asked to be excused from court while they were shown. His request was refused, so he sat with his back to the screen during the viewing.

Adelson went into such meticulous detail in describing the injuries that he took up an entire day in establishing how the victim had met her death. He was then cross-examined equally meticulously by Corrigan on almost every point of his evidence.

The defence lawyer made much of the fact that Adelson had not examined by microscope samples of the blood from Marilyn's face, had made no analysis of the stomach contents and had failed to ascertain whether or not she had been raped. Corrigan's reason for bringing up these points was his assertion that Adelson had been told by the police that Marilyn had been bludgeoned to death and had not bothered to look for any other cause. According to Corrigan she could equally well have been poisoned, but Adelson denied accepting any suggestions by the police, though he gave no reason for not having carried out a further autopsy.

Corrigan's cross-examination of Adelson also took an entire day, which annoyed Judge Blythin. He accused the lawyer of trying to lengthen the proceedings by irrelevant questioning and attempting to cloud the issue. It was by then Friday, and the judge said that if Corrigan did not bring his examination to a speedy conclusion he was prepared to sit all night and continue into Saturday. On Corrigan's promise to finish his questions on Monday the court adjourned for the week-end. On the Monday, with some reluctance, Corrigan ended his cross-examination of the pathologist without having made very many points in his client's favour.

The first witness to take the stand on the Tuesday was Don Ahern, the Sheppards' great friend. He testified that Sam and Marilyn were a devoted couple, and told how Marilyn had sat on Sam's lap during the evening while they were watching television. He said that the relationship between the couple seemed good, and that never in all the years he had known Sheppard had he ever seen him lose his temper.

Nancy Ahern, examined next, was less convincing about the attitude of Sheppard to his wife. She seemed somewhat reluctant to testify, but finally gave it as her opinion that most of the affection was on Marilyn's side. She also mentioned that she had been told by a third party, a Dr Chapman, that Sheppard had confided in him that he was seriously thinking of getting a divorce from Marilyn on the ground that she had 'admirers' and was not sufficiently 'sexually aggressive'. Naturally enough, Corrigan objected strongly to this hearsay evidence, for Dr Chapman was not a witness, but Judge Blythin over-ruled the defence and the testimony was allowed to remain on record.

Spencer Houk, the mayor of Bay Village, was next to take the stand, and told how he had been awakened at 5.45 a.m. by a telephone call from Sheppard and how he and his wife had rushed over to the house. Obviously uncomfortable and ill at ease, he said that immediately after the discovery of the body he had suggested to Sheppard that if he had really done it everyone would understand that this was in a fit of rage. Sheppard had been annoyed at the suggestion and insisted on his innocence. Indeed, he went further and reminded Spencer Houk that he himself could be a suspect if the police came to hear that he had been over-friendly with Marilyn and had long been one of her admirers.

Houk's wife, Esther, described the events of the morning at the Sheppard house, and repeated a conversation with Sheppard some weeks earlier, in connection with a suspected insurance fraud. The doctor had said how easy it was to simulate a head injury and how difficult to prove it false. This gave strength to the prosecution view that that was exactly what Sheppard had done to himself, and the defence was not overjoyed at Esther Houk's later testimony that Sam and Marilyn frequently had bitter arguments stemming mainly from her husband spending large sums on fast cars, such as the Jaguar, while begrudging his wife money to buy new furniture and a washing-machine.

A good deal of factual evidence came from the Bay Village policeman, Fred Drenkhan, who produced a large number of black-and-white photographs showing the scene of the murder and its surroundings. Drenkhan had also interviewed Sheppard in hospital, where he had been able to give only a very hazy description of his assailant. In particular Drenkhan had enquired about the T-shirt Sheppard had been wearing when the Aherns had left at midnight but which had vanished by the time he, Drenkhan, arrived at the house. Sheppard had said he had no idea. Drenkhan admitted in evidence that he did not believe Sam's story, as there was no evidence at all of a prowler in the district that night, no sign of forcible entry, and Sheppard had not used or picked up any weapon to protect himself. There also seemed little sign of burglary. Except the few bureau drawers that had been pulled out, and some general disorder, nothing of value had been taken. In answer to Corrigan, the policeman admitted that though he himself had arrested Sam on 30th July, the authorities were still looking for further evidence at the time.

Most of Drenkhan's evidence was confirmed by the next witness, Police Chief Eaton, who told of ordering the lake to be dragged in an attempt to find the murder weapon. Nothing suspicious was found. When Corrigan attempted to cross-examine the Chief on why the police had retained the keys of the house and refused access to the defence, the judge intervened and pronounced the question out of order.

The most effective witness for the prosecution was undoubtedly the coroner, Dr Samuel Gerber, who was to be in the witness-box for the next three days. Spare and white-haired, he had what has been described as an almost evangelical zeal to see Sheppard convicted and was a formidable opponent for the equally dedicated Corrigan.

It was Gerber who first described the murder weapon as 'a surgical instrument' because of blood marks on the pillow where, he said, the weapon had been placed for a short time after the murder. There was never any direct evidence that a surgical instrument had been used, and Gerber was quite unable to describe what sort of surgical instrument it might have been. The use of these words was unfortunate, to say the least, for Sam. Corrigan tried to get the offending words deleted from the record, but once again Judge Blythin disagreed, and 'a surgical instrument' was from then on closely associated with the murder weapon.

Gerber also maintained that the Sheppard family had obstructed him in his efforts to question Sam in hospital soon after the murder, and that he was forced to obtain a subpoena before he could finally interview him properly on 8th July.

Corrigan himself did not help his client by frequently losing his temper during his cross-examination of the coroner. The judge was forced to tell the jury to disregard

Corrigan's behaviour, and the defence lawyer and the prosecution almost came to blows when Corrigan, on the subject of Sheppard's wish for a divorce, sneeringly asked Gerber if he himself were not a divorced man? Once again the judge ordered the question to be struck out, the prosecution pointing out that there was no reason for the question, and that in any case the fundamental difference between Marilyn Sheppard and the former Mrs Gerber was that Mrs Gerber was still alive!

Things were a little quieter the next day during the examination of Detective Robert F. Schottke of the Cleveland homicide squad, the first member of the Cleveland police to question Sheppard officially a few days after the murder. He told the court of a statement Sheppard had made to him on 10th July in which he mentioned three other men who had been rebuffed by Marilyn after paying too much attention to her. The names of these would-be lovers were never revealed, but it was Sheppard's contention that one of these could have come to the house and murdered his wife after being refused once again. In the statement he also mentioned a wrist-watch that he had bought for Susan Hayes when he met her in Los Angeles. She had been invited to a dinner-party Sam had arranged for some doctors and their wives, and had somehow lost her watch. As she was present at Sheppard's invitation, he thought the least he could do was to buy her another one, but had not told Marilyn. When, later, Marilyn had discovered a receipt for this watch she had become upset, but had eventually accepted Sam's story.

Schottke also mentioned that Sheppard had been asked to undergo a lie-detector test, but had refused on the advice of his lawyers. Though the evidence from such a lie-detector test would not have been admissable in court, the detective wanted him to take it because, according to him, Sheppard had given three different versions of the events surrounding the discovery of his wife's body. Schottke's evidence on this point was cancelled out by the evidence of the next witness, Deputy Sheriff Rossbach, who had been with Schottke on each occasion he had questioned Sheppard. Rossbach insisted that Sheppard had kept to virtually the same story on each occasion.

There was similar contradictory evidence concerning the presence or absence of finger-prints. The first expert on this subject, Detective Michael Grabowski, said he failed to find a single finger-print anywhere in the house and was of the opinion that all surfaces had been wiped clean. This view was strengthened by his discovery of abrasion marks on smooth surfaces consistent with them having been wiped with a coarse cloth. But another colleague of Grabowski, using a different method, said he had found Sam's thumb-print on the head-board of Marilyn's bed, though this, as the defence was quick to point out, could have been made long before the murder simply by Sheppard bending over and perhaps kissing his wife goodnight.

Evidence was also heard regarding the drops of blood found on the coverlet of Sheppard's bed and continuing down the stairs. All this proved was that after the killing the murderer had come downstairs again, which was patently obvious, but certainly did not connect Sheppard with the crime. Once again Corrigan annoyed the judge by demanding photographs of the blood-spots, which the witness did not have with him, and asked for an adjournment while they were obtained. At first the judge refused, but Corrigan reminded him that he was fighting for a man's life. After remarking dryly that this was not the only murder-case going on in the State of Ohio, the judge relented and the adjournment was granted. But it was obvious that Judge Blythin was getting very tired of Corrigan and his tactics and openly accused him of being unfair to the jury and everyone else in court by 'making too much of a ritual of everything'.

To a certain extent the same accusation could be levelled at the prosecution, though the judge never censured them for it. At times their evidence seemed both pointless and inconclusive, as, for example, when a woman police-laboratory technician said she had examined Sheppard's trousers and had found sand in the turn-ups. However, no attempt had been made to match this sand with that on the beach where Sheppard said he had lapsed into unconsciousness after the chase; and even had this been done, it would have added little to the overall picture. This was probably why the police had taken no further action in identifying the beach sand, which raises the question why they sought to introduce it into the evidence in the first place.

Various other minor witnesses were called by the prosecution to underpin their evidence, which to many seemed extraordinarily flimsy. In order to substantiate a charge of first-degree murder, it must be shown that the deed was premeditated. It was therefore necessary to prove that Sam had *picked up a weapon* prior to going upstairs and murdering his wife. The Sheppards' maid, who lived out, was brought to court to testify whether any such potential instrument was missing from the Sheppard house when the police took her there a few days after the murder. She said she could not remember. Of more value was her evidence regarding the locking of the lake door at night. She said that as she frequently arrived at the house before the Sheppards were up, it was customary to leave the door unlocked during the night. This was a bonus for the defence, and explained why, if an intruder had come to the house, there was no sign of forcible entry.

Sheppard's missing T-shirt featured in the evidence given by Cyril M. Lipaj, a full-time Village Bay policeman at the time of the murder. He said he had found such a shirt near the shore when the police were dragging the lake. It was of a large size and had no blood-stains on it, and Sheppard had later agreed that it could possibly be his. But he had never

211

been shown the garment, and the prosecution took no further action in what could possibly have been an important piece of evidence.

The final prosecution witness was Susan Hayes, the alleged girl-friend of Sam Sheppard previously employed at the Bay View Hospital. Obviously under a great deal of strain, she recalled how she and the doctor had had sexual intercourse on several occasions while she worked at the hospital, sometimes in an upper room and sometimes in Sheppard's parked car. These episodes had taken place from 1952 until she finally left in 1954. When Sheppard had gone to the medical convention in Los Angeles he had contacted her and subsequently slept with her every night during his week's stay in the city. He had certainly given her presents, including a watch and a gold ring with her initials on it, but there was nothing more to it than that. He had once mentioned the possibility of divorcing Marilyn, but never of marrying her, and though he had written to her on four occasions none of these letters was in particularly loving terms.

Needless to say the press loved Susan, who was twenty-four years old and highly photogenic, and gave her the ritual 'scarlet woman' treatment reserved for such witnesses. Her picture appeared in the press from coast to coast, and for a day or two her face became almost as familiar in the press and on television as that of Sheppard himself. But what was her real value to the prosecution? All that had been proved was that Sheppard had been consistently unfaithful to his wife for some years and had later lied to the police about his relationship with the girl. The attitude of the press, however, implied that Sheppard was on trial not for murder but for immorality. But murder it was, said the prosecution, and with the testimony of Susan Hayes their case came to an end.

The first action of the defence, after the prosecution had completed its evidence, was to appeal to the judge that there was no case to answer and that the charge should be dismissed. Corrigan contended that a prima-facie case had not been established, and that even if all the prosecution's case were accepted it in no way proved the guilt of his client.

He went through the statement of witnesses heard to date, giving particular attention to the vague evidence regarding the T-shirt and stressing the fact that because a man was contemplating divorce and had had a long-standing extra-marital affair it did not make him a murderer.

The prosecution, in turn, made much of Sheppard's conflicting and incredible stories' and scoffed at the idea of a 'mysterious stranger' being anywhere near the Sheppard house that night. There was no doubt at all that Marilyn had been murdered and murdered in a house in which her husband had been the only other adult present.

These arguments took all day and the judge said he would give his decision the following morning. When he did so, it was to announce that, in his opinion, there *was* a case to answer.

It was now up to Corrigan to present the evidence for the defence. His first witness was Sam's older brother, Dr Stephen Sheppard, who proved to be somewhat aggressive and hostile and caused Corrigan some embarrassment. His main dispute was with the evidence given by Dr Hexter, the physician who had testified that Sam's injuries could well have been self-inflicted. Stephen Sheppard, as an experienced surgeon, had examined his brother carefully and was firmly convinced that the injuries to his neck, including the dislocation of a vertebra, the injuries to his face and the diminution of reflexes in the eye and limbs could not possibly have been caused by the accused himself. With the corroborative evidence of a top neurologist, Dr Charles Elkins, the medical evidence was so convincing that the prosecution, in their cross-examination of Stephen, were forced to mount a rearguard action and suggest the somewhat bizarre theory that if Sheppard's injuries were really so serious they probably came about through him trying to commit suicide in a fit of remorse!

There was also the curious matter of the position of the body when first seen, and the later photographs. Stephen Sheppard was quite certain that when he had seen the body at 6.20 a.m. Marilyn's pyjama-top was pulled up under her armpits, exposing her chest, and both arms were flung out sideways. Yet police photographs taken soon afterwards showed the pyjama-top pulled down, with one hand across her chest. The position of the legs was also changed, as was later confirmed by Sam's other brother, Richard, who had seen the body soon after Stephen. The implication of the defence was that the police had interfered with the body between its discovery and photographing, but the matter was not pursued in court and never subsequently clarified.

The defence had only a few minor witnesses apart from the medical brothers, and the climax of the trial was the appearance in the witness-box of Sheppard himself. He had a gruelling three days, but never varied substantially from his original account of the events of 3rd July. On his relationship with his wife he was on less firm ground, contending that he loved her dearly though admitting the occasional squabbles common to most married couples. He was vehement in his assertion that he had never considered divorce. On the question of his alleged meanness in respect of the new washing-machine, he said that his wife had bought this unknown to him, and had used money that he had set aside to pay the premium on a new insurance policy.

His version of how he had been treated by the police after his arrest caused a certain amount of disquiet. He accused them of subjecting him to 'third-degree' questioning more fitting to a Communist state, and of persistently lying to him about the evidence they had collected against him. This the police strenuously denied, offering to bring into court, to testify on oath, every policeman who had ever interrogated the accused. The offer was not taken up, which was perhaps unfortunate, as there was little doubt that the police had treated Sheppard harshly from the beginning and displayed an obvious hostility towards him, as Detective Schottke's own testimony had previously demonstrated.

In their cross-examination of Sheppard the prosecution made much of his sexual adventures, in particular his affair with Susan Hayes. Corrigan several times objected to this line of questioning, claiming that it had nothing whatever to do with the charge of murder and, in addition, was humiliating to Miss Hayes. But Judge Blythin once again opposed Corrigan. He said, 'When this gentleman is accused of murdering his wife, certainly his relations with other women are material,' and allowed the questioning to continue. Whether material or not, the prosecution made the most of it, for they did not have a great deal of direct evidence to go on. Sheppard himself remained reasonably calm throughout, but unfortunately did not impress the jury very favourably, exhibiting a certain amount of arrogance and sometimes giving the impression that, as a doctor, he was socially far removed from these unpleasant proceedings in court.

On 17th December, just two months after it began, the trial came to an end. Judge Blythin addressed the jury on their duties, giving them five alternative verdicts to choose from. These were:

1. First-degree murder.
2. First-degree murder with mercy.
3. Second-degree murder.
4. Manslaughter.
5. Not Guilty.

The jury retired, and at the end of four hours returned with a verdict of murder in the second degree. The judge thereupon announced a sentence of imprisonment for life, which enraged Corrigan. He insisted that the judge should not have pronounced sentence until he had heard if a new trial was to be demanded. He so forgot himself in court as to shout at Judge Blythin, 'I object to the way the court has conducted this entire case.'

Corrigan was immediately censured by Blythin, but then compounded the offence by trying to argue with the jury about its verdict. This time the judge was at his most severe, and Corrigan finally apologized to the court.

Sheppard was led away. One of the most controversial trials in American legal history had come to its end, fanned by a hostile press and including extraordinary court-room scenes which remain a disgrace to the American legal system.

This was by no means the end of the affair. A motion requesting a new trial was delivered to the court on 23rd December, based mainly on the grounds that the case had been heard by a local jury bound to have been influenced by local feeling and comment and by the hostility of the media. On 3rd January 1955 this application was denied in a lengthy document from Judge Blythin in which he said that as press and television coverage of the case had been nationwide, it seemed to him that the Cleveland jury was influenced no more than any other jury would have been.

The Sheppard family had been allowed back into the house by the police two days after Sam's conviction. They immediately hired a forensic expert, who, after examining the premises, claimed to have found fresh evidence, mainly concerned with the blood-spots, and supposedly proving Sam's innocence. As a result of this Sam's lawyers made an application to the Ohio District Court on two grounds: first, the original argument of local prejudice and press hostility, and secondly the new findings at the house. At this court three judges sat, but unanimously turned down the request for a fresh trial.

The next move was an appeal to the Ohio Supreme Court,

which was heard in April 1956. Six judges listened to a review of the case and finally came to the conclusion that the conviction should stand, though this decision was arrived at by a majority of four to two. There is evidence that the court had some sympathy for Sheppard and the judgement handed down began with the following much-quoted words:

Mystery and murder, society, sex, and suspense were combined in this case in such a manner as to intrigue and captivate the public fancy to a degree perhaps unparalled in recent annals. Throughout the pre-indictment investigation, the subsequent legal skirmishes and the nine-week trial, circulation-conscious editors catered to the insatiable interest of the American public in the bizarre. Special seating facilities for reporters and columnists representing local papers and all the major news-services were installed in the court-room. Special rooms in the Criminal Court buildings were equipped for broadcasters and telecasters. In this atmosphere of a 'Roman holiday' for the news media Sam Sheppard stood trial for his life.

Nevertheless, the court refused the application. There remained only the United States Supreme Court to which Sheppard and his lawyers could turn.

This was not an automatic matter, and the Supreme Court could make its own decision whether it heard the case or not. Though Corrigan petitioned the court forcibly on the validity of Sheppard's trial in a hostile atmosphere, the Supreme Court, in a decision reached in October 1956, stated its unwillingness to re-open the case. It looked as if Sam had reached the end of the road.

In the following year, 1957, two events took place which had the effect of re-kindling the Sheppard affair in the public mind, though in fact it had scarcely waned and was being argued about as thoroughly as ever. First was a 'confession' by a 23-year-old convict called Donald Wedler, in prison in Florida, that he had murdered Marilyn Sheppard. Confessions of this kind were not new (there had been twenty-five so far) but in this instance it was investigated rather more thoroughly, and for a time it looked as if the case would be re-opened. Wedler said he was in the Village Bay area on the night in question, had been 'high' on drugs and could have killed Marilyn after walking into the doctor's unlocked home in search of fresh supplies. He could give no details of his supposed action, and the lie-detector test he was given proved inconclusive. The matter was eventually dropped and Wedler, after a brief spate of notoriety, was returned to Florida to complete his sentence.

But the Wedler incident also coincided with the intervention of an extraordinary organization calling itself 'The Court of Last Resort'. This was the brainchild of the former lawyer and celebrated crime-writer, Erle Stanley Gardner, widely acclaimed as the creator of Perrry Mason. This 'court' consisted of various wealthy men, including several lawyers such as the redoubtable Marshall Houts, and the well-known private investigator, Raymond Schindler. Its purpose was to investigate apparent miscarriages of justice in criminal cases, when all other means had failed. One of Gardner's co-founders had been the magazine-publisher Harry Steeger, who gave the 'court's' various investigations a good deal of publicity. This proved not to be to the advantage of the Court of Last Resort, for when it approached Judge Blythin for a re-hearing of the case via the Attorney-General of Ohio, the following dusty answer was received:

> I believe the Attorney-General of Ohio should immediately take steps in the name of the state to deny any individual or group the right or privilege to designate themselves as a Court of Last Resort or court under any other name in Ohio. We have only those courts established under our constitution and laws. To come in as a Court of Last Resort after the Ohio and United States

Supreme Courts have acted is to place itself above those courts. This court is acting in the interest of increasing the circulation of a national magazine.

Though no further action was taken by the Court of Last Resort, during the years that followed several unsuccessful appeals were made to the Supreme Court for a re-trial of the Sheppard case, or for his early release on parole. Finally, in July 1964, as the result of an enormous amount of work done by F. Lee Bailey, a young lawyer hired by the Sheppard family, a petition for habeas corpus was permitted to be presented to Federal Judge Carl Weinmann. This petition was based on twenty-three charges that the case had not been properly conducted ten years earlier. It included an affidavit from a woman reporter claiming that during an interview with Judge Blythin before the commencement of the original trial, he had said, 'It is an open-and-shut case. Sam Sheppard is as guilty as hell.' Another complaint was that the jury, while in retirement to discuss their verdict, had been allowed to make unmonitored telephone calls from the hotel to their friends and relations.

The upshot of the matter was that Judge Weinmann handed down a judgement in which he said that he had found five separate violations of the prisoner's constitutional rights, and that 'the trial could only be viewed as a mockery of justice'.

He ordered immediate release from custody on a $10,000 bond pending a re-trial.

After an interval of ten years it took some time to re-assemble the original witnesses. Some, like Judge Blythin, were dead, and it was not until October 1966 that the second trial started. F. Lee Bailey and William Corrigan represented the defence and once again the chief prosecution witness was the Coroner, Dr Samuel Gerber. This time, however, Gerber seemed less sure of his facts, in particular his contention that the bloody marks on Marilyn's pillow had been made by a surgical instrument.

The trial took three weeks (the first week spent in ensuring that the jury were all comparatively young people) and on 16th November 1966 they returned a verdict of not guilty. After ten years in prison and two on bail, Sam Sheppard was a free man again.

Unfortunately, Sheppard was also a broken man. His attempts to rehabilitate himself were unsuccessful. Within days of his release he married for a second time, not to Susan Hayes (as the more romantic members of the community would have liked), but to a glamorous German girl called Ariane Tebbenjohanns who had corresponded with him regularly all the time he had been in prison, and who had come to America immediately on his release. But it was too late. Sheppard became an alcoholic despite the efforts of his new wife, and the marriage ended in divorce in 1968.

Though Sam had been re-instated to the medical register in 1967 he was not in a fit state to take advantage of it. In a pathetic effort to cash in on his notoriety he became a small-time professional wrestler and married Colleen Strickland, the twenty-year-old daughter of his trainer, in October 1969.

On 6th April 1970 Sam Sheppard was found dead in bed from an overdose of drink and drugs. He was forty-six. Predictably the press and television covered the funeral, though few members of his immediate family were present, his brother Stephen and his son Chip being away in Europe and unable to return in time.

So ended one of the most bizarre murder cases in American history. There are some who maintain that Sheppard's original mis-trial and conviction, and even his own death, were the result of the hostile attitude of the media. The American press naturally discounts this view, and upholds its 'freedom' to report anything considered to be in the public interest.

But the fundamental question has never been satisfactorily settled: 'Who killed Marilyn Sheppard?'

Undoubtedly there will always remain a question-mark over a case in which the same man was both convicted and acquitted of murdering his wife.